HOW I MADE OVER ONE MILLION DOLLARS SELLING CARS

A Great Career for An Uneducated Slouch

By

William Heussner

This book is dedicated to:

My wife Beth and son Grant who have stuck with me and supported me in my pursuit of happiness via the automotive retail sales lifestyle. I Love you both more than words could express. And to my father in law, Jim Schirott, for inspiring me to write a book.

Contents

Introduction

Congratulations on purchasing "HOW I MADE OVER ONE MILLION DOLLARS SELLING CARS."

This book is about my career selling cars, how I earned over one million dollars and how I did it.

I will explain in detail, how I have consistently earned an income level only 5.4% of the US population earn per year (according to US Census data from July/2018) and done it without a college degree. Due to my lack of a college degree is why I refer to myself as an "uneducated slouch."

I will write about why I chose to be in the car business, my outlook on what it takes to be a successful car salesperson as well as the attitude and methods I've utilized to be successful.

I don't claim to be the greatest car salesperson ever although I can tell you what I have accomplished during my car sales career – I've ranked in the top 100 sales consultants in the US for a major luxury vehicle brand. I've won "Salesman of the Year" three times at one of the largest luxury car dealerships in the State of Illinois. I've also earned the top tier sales award 9 times for the brand I sell so I have a nice gold ring with 9 diamonds in it. Last, but not least, I have earned over ONE MILLION DOLLARS SELLING CARS!

By reading this book you will learn how I accomplished a successful and rewarding career in automotive retail sales.

I'm living proof that even an uneducated slouch can earn over one million dollars in the car business and the information provided in this book explains how I did it.

As the old saying goes, "time is money" so start reading and get your car sales career started so you can earn some serious money! The sooner you get started and implement the things I write about, the sooner you will be able to look back on your career and possess a tremendous feeling of accomplishment, knowing you have earned over ONE MILLION DOLLARS SELLING CARS! If you are already selling cars or have been for a long time, I hope you pick up a new idea or two that helps you close more deals and earn more repeat and referral clients.

Chapter 1 – Attitude is Everything

Before I dive into how important attitude is to be successful in the automotive retail sales profession, I would like to tell a little bit about myself and how I ended up in the car business. I was born in a small town in southern Wisconsin. My father was an auto factory worker and my mother was a stay at home mom and accomplished artist. I have three older sisters and one younger brother, so my parents had to be very frugal to ensure we had decent clothes to wear, food on the table and a roof over our heads. My father had a lot of common sense and an incredible work ethic and my mother is extremely creative. Mom also worked very hard, raising 5 children is no small job. Not to mention, making time to generate some of the most beautiful artwork I've ever seen. Dad passed away from cancer in 2013 however he had a great sense of humor and so does Mom. I believe a great sense of humor is probably the single most important trait one must have to get through life in general. I'm lucky and grateful to have been raised by them and have learned so much from them. Most of what I've accomplished is due to their influence, as well as my four siblings. The "GREAT NEWS" is that you don't have to be born with these traits or have been environmentally conditioned to have these traits. You can learn them from me in this book!

So, how did I end up in the car business? During high school I decided that after graduation I would go to a local technical college for architectural drafting. I was a good artist, having been exposed my whole life to my Mom doing art in our home. She would get us kids involved and always had art supplies around – paint and brushes, crayons, markers, pencils, etc…. Mom even made homemade play dough and paper mâché for us to work with. I never earned less than an "A" grade in any art class I ever took during school and I had excellent penmanship so I thought architectural drafting was something I could be good at doing. I still have excellent lettering skills but don't worry, you don't need good lettering, penmanship skills or artistic talent to be a great car salesperson.

The only other class I got "A" grades in was gym class. From a young age I really liked sports and played sports throughout my childhood and high school. Dad always told me baseball was my best sport however my Grandfather (Grandpa Knight) introduced me to the game of golf and I loved it! So, once I found out you could golf every day for free if you joined the high school golf team I was done with baseball! Mom did work part time for a local insurance agent once all of us kids became self-sufficient and when the insurance office got their new issue of an instructional golf magazine every month, she would bring the previous issue home for me to read. I never took a golf lesson although I read every issue of that golf magazine and practiced what I read. I would take the hand me down clubs and scuffed golf balls Grandpa Knight gave me and go across Whitewater Avenue to the local National Guard Armory lawn to practice what I learned. Mom and Dad didn't have much extra money, so I wasn't able to benefit from being a member of a country club or taking private golf lessons from a club pro. Mom and Dad didn't have enough money to buy me new golf clubs either. I needed a respectable set of clubs to fit in on the golf team, so I worked on one of my buddy's Dad's poultry farm catching chickens and shoveling chicken shit for $3.00 per hour. I saved enough money for a decent set of used clubs, some new golf spikes, and joined the golf team. The important point of this whole rambling is that I made it happen because I had the right attitude! I was determined and that is a character trait you do need to be a great car salesperson or selling anything for that matter. Determination isn't something you need to be born with. If there is something you want to accomplish just decide in your mind that you are going to do what it takes to get the job done and do it! It's that simple. I do want to be clear that I was far from the best golfer on the team. In fact, I didn't even earn a varsity letter since I played junior varsity matches but I did accomplish my goal of free golf and I enjoyed every round.

That leads me to another example of having the right attitude to accomplish a goal. When I was a kid in small town Wisconsin, I thought the coolest kids in town were the high school kids with their "F" letter jackets. I wanted one so I could be what I thought was cool (now I know that there are far more important things in life than being a jock wearing a letter jacket.) The point here is that I made up my mind that I was going to earn that "F" jacket! My absolute favorite sport was football and it was a real gut-punch once I figured out that I didn't have the raw talent to be a professional football player. In fact, I knew going into my Junior year on the Varsity squad that I wasn't even going to be a starter, even on special teams (kicking and punting units for those of you who don't know football.) I'd like to think it was because we were so loaded with talent as a team that I wasn't bad, we just had a lot of great football players. So, how was I going to get on the field to earn my "F" jacket? You needed to play in a minimum number of quarters to earn the jacket. Well, we didn't have a place kicker so at the beginning of "two a day" summer practice, Coach asked "Who wants to try out for place kicker?" I jumped at the opportunity and what do you know, I got the job! The point here is that I knew what I wanted to accomplish, and I was willing to adjust strategy to get it done. This is the attitude you need to have – determination, courage and a willingness to try a different approach to accomplish the same goal. As my old buddy Ole once said: "If whatever you're doing isn't working, try anything else!"

So, after high school, I went to drafting school and came out of it with three sets of plans (blueprints) that looked like a professional architect drew them and landed a job for a well-known architect in Madison, WI. He designed some cool stuff – a major botanical garden, a unique Swiss styled hotel, and a sort of prairie style park shelter to name a few of his projects. The problem was that I didn't have any construction experience and after two months I was fired because I was bothering the architect with too many questions. Another gut-punch! This was a big blow to my psyche because my plan didn't come together. I worked very hard, going through the tech school drafting program and working second shift and summer jobs while doing it. It took a lot of effort, only to feel like it was all wasted. Anyway, I got a job in a furniture assembly factory just down the block from my apartment I was renting, and they promised me they would promote me into their drafting department as soon as there was an opening. Well, after 9 months, the drafting opportunity still hadn't opened so I got a job in another factory that paid a little better than the furniture assembly gig. Ironically, it was another furniture factory. Here again, what I was doing wasn't working, so I tried something else! My thought at the time was to move home and save some money, try to get into a University and earn my bachelor's degree. I really wasn't sure what I wanted to study though.

I took another factory job at a company that formulated and manufactured industrial chemicals. It was an interesting business and the owner paid well and rewarded hard work with consistent raises and promotions. It was hard, hazardous and dirty work but it paid better than the furniture factories. Covering a period of about three years, I was promoted from packager, to batch maker, to shop foreman, to quality control technician, to lab technician and eventually into sales. Not bad for an uneducated slouch, but I did work my ass off. Split it right down the middle! Ha, ha. That is a one-liner I learned from my first boss at the chemical plant. Early on, during my time with this company there was a retirement party for one of the long-time salesmen and it appeared he had done very well for himself with his career there. I came to this conclusion by the big shiny luxury car he drove, the gold rings adorning his fat fingers and the large gold chain around his neck with a big gold medallion hanging down from it. The gold and big fancy luxury car weren't my style however I thought to myself that I sure wouldn't mind having enough money to buy a nice fishing boat and retire comfortably someday. I thought, maybe I could become a salesman for this company and have a nice retirement party like this and ride off into the sunset on my fishing boat. I expressed an interest to the owner, and he seemed to think I could be in sales, but he said I needed to go to a local junior college to take an accounting class and a business class. If I earned A's he would give me a shot at the sales job. Here again, I had the guts to throw my hat in the ring and take a shot at it. I took advantage of the opportunity in front of me and worked hard to accomplish my goal. I got the A's and started selling chemicals.

Toward the end of my 8 years selling chemicals I could clearly see that the end was near. I had a feeling I was going to be terminated. I won't divulge why things were going south but I started thinking: What am I going to do to earn a good living with no college degree when this job ends? I had a two year non-compete contract I had signed and was informed by my father in law who was an attorney that it was indeed enforceable because the company paid me to sign it. I had to do something other than sell the only industry I had been involved in for the last 13 years. The only real world, practical experience I possessed (professionally – not counting washing dishes, catching chickens and shoveling chicken shit, factory assembly work, clerking at a convenience store, or janitorial work) was in this industry that I was legally prevented from participating in for two years. Driving to a sales call one day and stuck in very heavy Chicago traffic, I thought to myself – wow, there sure are a lot of cars on the road! Almost every adult person in America has a car. So many cars! Maybe selling cars would be a good way to earn a living? I could just go to a dealership every day and wait for someone to show up and buy a car and while I was waiting, I could work on my degree through an online University. At this point in time, I decided that should something happen to end the chemical sales gig, I would become a car salesperson.

Soon after thinking about selling cars for a living if anything should happen with the chemical sales job, it happened. One day I was called into the conference room by my boss with the Director of Sales and they fired me.

Another gut-punch! Even though I knew things were heading this direction it was still a heavy blow because I had invested 13 years of hard work and dedication to that company and I was on the street. Not homeless on the street, but out of good paying job. They did give me a nice 4-month severance package of full pay and benefits. I thought that was fair, but I was still out of a good paying job.

So, the hunt for a car sales job began! I was living in WI however I was dating a girl from the Chicago suburbs at the time (now my wife) so I thought why not look for something close to her in the Chicago area. I interviewed with three dealerships in one day and was offered a job by two of them on the spot. Both dealerships that offered me the job were your run of the mill car brands, produced by the company my Dad worked for, for almost 40 years. I had to stay loyal to that company since they were the company that took care of my family, as a product of my Dad's almost 40 years of hard work and dedication to them. The third dealership was a luxury brand dealership of the same company Dad worked for, as well as 6 other new car franchises at three different locations and they didn't offer me the job on the spot. I interviewed with two different managers at two different locations and they said we'll get back to you. The following day I hadn't heard anything so I followed up with one of the managers who I interviewed with and he said - "Could you start Monday?" I said - "Yes sir, what time should I be there?" and so it began! A good take away here is that you need to create your own luck. I didn't wait for them to get back to me, I got back to them and it was that simple. My father in law told me once that "Half the battle is showing up." I think showing up means several different things – making the decision and having the courage to overcome your fear of failure and trying new things, taking calculated risks, applying for the job you don't think you're qualified for, being on time (I actually show up 15 minutes early because there was a famous football coach who said if you're not 15 minutes early you're late), and timely follow up. Then of course is the obvious meaning of "showing up" – excellent attendance! If you're not in the showroom or on the job, how are you going to sell cars or get the job done?

A few things I hope you take away from the previous paragraphs and continue to think about as you proceed through this book are that you can't let gut-punching adversity keep you down. You need to be flexible with your game plan, determined to succeed, resilient and work hard!

So now that I've already explained a few of the attitudes I think you need to possess or develop to be successful in car sales (and life in general) I'd like to explain what I think is the most important attitude - a great sense of humor. Why do I think a great sense of humor is #1? It is because not only in car sales, but life in general, if you're able to find humor in any situation you will generally smile and therefore, you will feel better than if you're not smiling. Very simple but true. For the same reason you need to make yourself smile, it will return massive gains to your long-term income if you are able to make your clients laugh and smile. Why? It's because if your clients are laughing and smiling then they will be happier and more likely to enjoy the interaction they have with you, vs. your competitor who is grumpy and providing "service with a snarl", instead of "service with a smile." That comment I just mentioned ("service with a snarl") still makes me laugh and smile and I've probably thought it or said it hundreds of times. I first heard it said by my long-time pal Ole who I have known since I was knee high to a grasshopper. Ole is one of the funniest people I've ever known. I quoted him previously and he may be credited further in this book with more one-liners I've learned from him. I won't repeat any of his Norwegian jokes because I'm not Norwegian and don't want to be insensitive. Ole is Norwegian so I think he can get away with telling those jokes.

Now I will provide a few examples of things I do to get my customers laughing and smiling. The very first and most important thing is to have a genuine, large smile on your face when greeting the client. At one training session early in my car sales career we had a training specialist from one of the top luxury hotel chains in the world, and they put a huge emphasis on first impression. As a 5-star luxury hotel, they must provide a luxury experience to their guests and they have perfected it, so I took to heart what they were telling us that day. Per Wikipedia, first impression is explained like this: "In psychology, a first impression is the event when one person first encounters another person and forms a mental image of that person." So, when I greet a client, I always try to focus on generating the biggest smile I can muster at the same time I'm making initial eye contact. When you initially meet someone, they form their overall opinion of you very quickly. I forget the actual number of seconds, but it is within seconds, not minutes. The first impression your client forms of you dictates how receptive they will be to buy a car from you (or whatever you are selling.) It doesn't necessarily mean you won't sell them a car however it does make them more likely to purchase from you as well as enjoy their interaction with you and return as a repeat client. In other words, the client will like you better and people are far more likely to buy from someone they like vs. someone they don't like. Very simple concept.

One trick I learned a long time ago and I think has been a huge part of my success is that when I initially greet a client, I think about how I feel when I see an old friend I haven't seen in a very long time. Sometimes I think of an old buddy I haven't seen for a very long time, or my brother Ben who I don't see often enough. Thinking about greeting them makes me happy and instantly brings a big smile to my face. Since I'm smiling huge, the client I'm greeting usually smiles back and it's a great tool in "breaking the ice." There is usually a lot of ice too since clients entering a car dealership are typically making the second largest expenditure of money they make in their life, second to home purchases. For this reason, many of them are very guarded, defensive and afraid of being "ripped off." If I greet them with a massive smile, they will feel the good vibes, be more likely to like me and therefore buy their second largest purchase in their life from me. If you don't have a brother or an old buddy to think of that make you smile, think about something that does make you happy and smile. Maybe a time when one of your children made you LOL, or a funny scene in a movie, or a comedian you like. One other critical factor of my greeting is I know I must be genuine in my greeting. People will sense it if I'm not genuine and putting on a phony smile. One thing that helps me ensure I'm genuine is knowing that roughly 9 out of 10 client interactions are going to be fun and I will be making a new friend, whether I sell them a car or not. Many times, even if I didn't get the sale, clients come back years later and tell me – "I should have bought from you last time." The one out of 10 clients you don't befriend are what one sales trainer along the way referred to as the "10 percenters." In other words, no matter what you do, 10 percent of the clients you assist will not be happy. I think the number is far less than 10 percent for me because of how I greet and treat my clients however on occasion, there is a customer that I can't satisfy or get to smile, no matter what I do. I don't judge these clients as bad people because I'm not in their shoes and don't know what sort of gut punches they might be going through in life. The takeaway from this paragraph should be to get your mind in a genuinely happy state when greeting clients and focus on the fact that most clients will appreciate your genuine happiness, buy from you, and be back to see you again.

One of my go to ways to get clients laughing is what I call the "hand slide" presentation. If you haven't ever seen the old game shows with the models that slide their hands below the prizes you wouldn't know what I'm talking about but it's funny stuff to me. I don't think many people think much about it when a professional model does the slow hand slide, however when I do it and I notice my customer smiling because they didn't expect a 220 lb car salesman with a scar on his nose and a bald spot on the side of his head doing it, I know I've made a favorable impression of myself with that one little gesture. I know it sounds corny and it is corny, but corny is funny. Funny makes people laugh or smile and therefore, they are happier and more likely to buy from you and become one of your loyal repeat clients.

Another one liner that works to get my clients smiling (because I'm a bit heavier than my 5'-11" frame should allow) is when I'm on a demonstration drive with my client and they ask me - "What is the 0-60 time?" I reply - "Well, it's a lot faster when I'm not in it!" I don't recall one client not laughing at that one, ever. Now that one should only be used if you're bigger than the client. You don't want to make your client feel self-conscious. Me on the other hand, I'm able to laugh at my overweightness (is that a real word?) and because I'm able to laugh at myself, I feel better. When I feel better, my clients feel the good vibes and they feel better too so they will want to buy from me vs. the "service with a snarl" sales consultant that I'm competing with. I truly believe that like a section of a magazine my Mom used to read said, "laughter is the best medicine."

One very important aspect of humor during a car sale is when to deploy it and when not to deploy it. I use it sparingly because if you're using too much humor you will lose credibility and the client will only see you as a goofball. You still need to present a very professional appearance, presentation and interaction with your clients, however injecting a bit of humor here and there lightens things up a bit, making your clients more comfortable with you vs. your competition. A little bit of well-timed humor goes a long way in making clients happy.

Another great way to make a client laugh is the old "I could write down a smaller number for you." When negotiating the figures and the customer is insisting on a lower price, say to them "I could write a smaller number for you" and then write the exact same price previously offered only much smaller than the first time. This one will almost always get the customer to smile, if not laugh out loud. This one is a great to utilize even with the most serious, toughest negotiating clients you will encounter.

You do need to be cautious though because I guess in theory the customer could become upset although I've never had a problem, only laughs and smiles.

The chair drop is another good one when you're faced with a tough negotiator. It works like this: The client is beating you up, working you for a lower price. Say to the client – "I could go lower for you." Then place your hand on the lever of your desk chair that lowers the height of the chair and push the lever, so your chair drops slowly to a lower position. This one has always been received with smiles and laughs by my clients however I still caution you to ensure the timing is right, so you don't upset the client. I give credit to one of my old managers for the chair drop and the smaller number lines. The guy I learned them from was a very funny guy and master of when to deploy humor during a car deal, and the loyalty of his customers was proof that happy clients are return clients. He had a huge following of loyal clients that loved him because he made the car buying process fun. So, not only in car sales, but whatever you're selling, make it fun and people will like you better than your competitors that don't make it fun. I've seen many salespeople come and go from the dealership I work at that have miserable, negative, grumpy, combative attitudes. They still sell cars, but they don't reap the long-term rewards of repeat clients because people don't want to deal with their "service with a snarl!"

Whether it's laughing with your clients, laughing at yourself, or any time it is appropriate and well timed, utilizing humor will make you and your clients happier. Happy clients are far more likely to be repeat clients, a huge reason I've been able to earn OVER ONE MILLION DOLLARS SELLING CARS!

The next attitude you need to have or develop is being positive. Car sales can be like a wicked mother in law, always trying to beat you down with adversity, however you can overcome it with a positive attitude! My positive attitude starts with preparing to go to work every morning. I shower, shave, trim my eyebrows, nose and ears if needed, and put on a pressed white cotton business shirt and tie and dress pants. I also make sure my shoes are comfortable and in good condition. After ruining three $300 pairs of dress shoes in my first 6 months in the business, I tried several different brands and styles of less expensive shoes and finally found bison leather loafers. I think I'm on my 7th pair in a row because they look great, are tough as a bison and the soles wear well. Pounding the pavement on the car lot, showing and fetching cars, is tough on shoes, especially in the northern climate of northern Illinois. The bison leather seems to be inherently resistant to the liberal use of salts being used to melt snow and ice we deal with here too. The salt in combination with the leather soles wearing out quickly is what took out the $300/pair shoes. I know firsthand how tough bison are because my father in law Jim raised a small heard of them as a retirement hobby. He started out with a bull and two cows and if I remember correctly, he built his herd up to 6 or 7 bison. After the last one broke through the fence he sold them off and I think he kept one for processing. I remember visiting one time and there were no more bison, just copious amounts of ground bison meat and jerky. Jim always said – "The bison are either happy or hamburger!" Now back to my writing of how important shoes are. I mention shoes because I have personally noticed many other salespeople wearing shoes that weren't right for them and they spend a lot of time thinking about and complaining about their shoes. Time that could have been spent focusing on what could be done to sell a car. If you're feet are uncomfortable it will be that much more difficult for you to stay positive. This also holds true for your clothing too. If your shirt is too tight or the sleeves are too long or too short or your pants are too tight you won't feel comfortable and that can deter you from maintaining a positive attitude. Your customers will also sense that you're uncomfortable and that will make them uncomfortable. Comfortable clients are happier clients! Another tip I learned from the 5-star hotel trainer was that people take notice of your fingernails and shoes and the impression they form of you is heavily dependent on those two things. So, keep your fingernails clean and trimmed and keep your shoes clean, polished and in presentable condition.

Many things that happen in life can give us a negative attitude. Your child is mad at you because you wouldn't let him have electronics time before 8:00 am, the wife is mad because you drank too many beers the night before, the dog hates you because you forgot to buy his rawhide chew toy, someone flipped you the bird during your morning commute. Whatever negative forces are trying to give you a negative attitude, leave them at the door when you arrive to work! What do I mean by this? It means that whatever adversity you have going on in your personal life, you must leave it behind you and forget about it when you walk through the showroom door in the morning. In fact, if I'm having a difficult personal issue, I leave it in my car! Before I get out of my car, I tell myself – "Time to forget about this B.S. and focus on selling a car!" Or, I will say to myself – "Don't sweat the small stuff." Another thing I like to do to put me in a better mood is music. When times are difficult, I have a few go to songs I listen to that brighten my mood and give me hope. You need to find a song or songs or something else that will assist you with getting your mind off the negative stuff you're dealing with. With that said, there are times that aren't that easy to just forget about. If you've lost a family member or friend and you're having a hard time dealing with it or very serious issues like that, you're better off seeking professional help and maybe taking some personal time off and/or bereavement time. That is just my humble opinion.

Negative coworkers and fellow salespeople are another negative force to avoid. Throughout my years in the car business I have experienced many other salespeople that hang around the coffee pot or the water cooler and spread negativity about how business is slow, how they lost this deal or that deal, and complain about difficult customers. I do my best to not expose myself to the negative vibes of other salespeople as this negativity will adversely affect me. I will get my cup of coffee or water and get back to my desk and get to work! I'm not rude to my coworkers, I just politely let them know I've got work to do. Even if you don't hang around the coffee pot or water cooler with them, they will also migrate to your desk and want to "shoot the bull" and that can be a big distraction and time waster. When one of my fellow salespeople approach me and are just hanging out to waste time I continue working – making phone calls, sending text messages and emails and they quickly get the idea that I'm not paying attention to them and they leave. It may sound rude however I will politely say to them soon after they approach – "Excuse me however I have to make this phone call" and they understand that I have work to do. I'm not against a little bit of socializing at work and I like joking around with coworkers a little bit, but I do my best to keep it to a minimum and avoid the negative coworkers because I'm determined to be positive and I know being exposed to the negativity will compromise my positivity.

I would say the biggest, most powerful of negative forces is the dreaded sales slump. I still struggle with staying positive during a slump however when I am in a slump, I remind myself that a hot streak is coming! If you stick with car sales long enough and do what you're supposed to do, along the way you will have mostly streaks of above average sales however occasionally you will experience a slump. I define a slump as a period of anywhere from 2 days to a week with few or no sales. When I'm in a slump I feel the best approach to get myself out of it is to work my way out of it. By that I mean go back and do the old saying – "The harder you work, the luckier you get!" It has proven true for me. Instead of making 20 phone calls a day, I will make 30. Instead of sending 10 emails, I will send 20. Instead of texting customers I'm working deals with or leads I'm following up on once per day, I will text them two or three times per day. When I deploy this strategy, whether the extra work I put in directly results in sales or not, the sales start to happen again. The sooner you accept the fact that car sales is streaky business, the better equipped you will be to deal with the dreaded sales slump when it happens. In fact, as I'm typing this it is January 30, 2019. Two days left in the first month of 2019 and I just delivered my 11th car for the month yesterday. I'm at home writing this book because the dealership closed our sales department due to a "polar vortex" that has dropped temperatures to -24F this morning. Anyway, through 1/23 I had only sold and delivered 3 cars for the entire month. I was in a slump so what did I do? I worked my way out of it by putting my nose to the grindstone and making more calls, more emails and more text messages. The extra effort did create at least two of the 8 sales I made in 6 days and I exceeded the first bonus level in a tough month hampered by snow and cold. I worked my way into a "hot streak!" In a normal month without winter weather slowing things down I would have had a great chance to sell 2-4 more cars and hit the second or third bonus level, plus 2-4 additional commissions, plus bonus money from the manufacturer for selling new cars.

It's been 6 days since I wrote the last paragraph. This book is a sideline to my everyday routine, so I haven't been able to write since it was -24F and the dealership was closed due to the bone stabbing cold weather. Well, we reopened for business the following day and my vehicle thermometer read -22F on my way into the dealership. I wasn't expecting to sell any cars that day. What customer in their right mind would come out and buy a car on a day like that? I knew one thing, if anyone was coming into the showroom on a day like this, they were a serious buyer and needed a car! Even though I wasn't expecting to sell any cars this day I still had the right mind set that I had a chance and I would give it maximum effort. At least I could make phone calls, send text messages and email customers to set up a quick start to February. My wife's job was closed, and my son's school was closed so they were able to stay home and enjoy the comforts of a well-insulated and heated home. I whipped up a bunch of vittles for them on Wednesday – Belgian waffles and thick cut hickory smoked bacon for breakfast, and roasted pork tenderloin, handmade spaetzle and gravy with steak mushrooms for dinner, so they had some nice leftovers to enjoy while I was at the dealership on Thursday in day two of the polar vortex.

Anyway, instead of sleeping in since I didn't have to get my boy Grant up and going, feed him breakfast, make his lunch and drop him off at school. I decided to maximize my effort and get my ass into the dealership early! That's right, instead of completely writing off the day as a waste of time because no customers would be coming in, I had a POSITIVE ATTITUDE and made the most out of it. Guess what happened? I sold two cars on the last day of January to make it 13 for the month. 13 cars in a month earn you the second bonus level at my dealership, so I increased my bonus by an additional $500 and I earned two more commissions. In addition, both deals were new vehicles, so it added another $300-$400 in bonus money (spiffs) from the manufacturer and at least $200 each in commission. The range in spiffs is because there are several criteria that need to be met for you to receive the full bonus amount. If you meet all the criteria you earn $200 per car once you sell 4 or more in one month. Add it all up and I earned an extra $1,300 (maybe more if the commissions are more than the minimum of $200) for the month on a day when the temperature was -22F when we opened and almost everything in the entire midwestern US was closed.

What was the point of all that rambling? I was trying to make the point that by having a positive attitude, finding opportunity in any situation, and working hard, you will get yourself out of the dreaded sales slump when it happens. Sales slumps will happen in the car business (I think any business for that matter) however if you stay the course, know there is light at the end of the tunnel and maximize your effort you will turn the slump into a hot streak! Oh yeah, I forgot to mention – I've started out February with 4 sales in three working days, so the hot streak has continued.

Now, what would have happened if I didn't get myself out of that three-week long January slump? Would I have been discouraged? I would absolutely be discouraged, and I have been there. I'm not going to B.S. you into thinking the car business is always like looking through rose-colored glasses and that you will be able to maintain a positive attitude your entire career however you have the choice to be positive or be negative. You need to choose positive and when you find yourself being negative, find ways to get positive! Be creative. Find opportunity in the face of adversity. Generate luck through hard work. These principals are simple but not easy, however you can do it if you put your mind to it and make it a point to have a POSITIVE ATTITUDE!

Another negative force that will try to bring you down are negative, grumpy, demanding clients, or the "ten percenters." I think whoever coined that phrase "ten percenters" might have had a bit of a bad attitude because when I really think about it, my occurrence of clients that I can't make happy is probably much less than 10%. I think it's lower for me because of how I interact with my clients, doing all the things I wrote in the previous paragraphs. I've seen quite a few salespeople over the years that have a combative attitude with clients throughout the sales process and they still sell cars, however very few of their customers come back as repeat clients. Have you noticed how many times in this book I've mentioned "repeat clients" already? Many times, I have greeted clients that entered the showroom with their "guns blazing", ready for a fight and determined to not let the evil car salesman gouge their eyeballs (and their pocketbook) out. Most of the time, by the time these clients leave the showroom, we part as good friends. One great way to lower your client's defenses is to show a genuine interest in them. It could be as simple as asking them about the logo on their shirt, jacket or hat. Most of the time, if someone is wearing an article of clothing with a logo, the logo is something to do with their career or job or is one of their hobby's or interests. Since people in general like talking about themselves, if you can get them talking about themselves and show a genuine interest in what they're saying, they will feel that genuine interest and be far more likely to like you. The more the client likes you, the more likely they are to buy from you and become a repeat client. You must be interested in other people to be a great car salesperson.

Another way to get your clients talking about themselves is to be observant of what is in or on their trade vehicle. Maybe ask them about a bumper sticker that is on their trade vehicle or maybe they have some other indicator of their interests in their vehicle – a box of golf balls, a shopping bag from a specialty shop, a personalized license plate frame or personalized license plate. Some of my best, most loyal repeat clients came into the dealership with their "guns blazing" however I was able to break down their defenses, be a friend and consequently sell them many cars. What you need to take away from this paragraph is to know you will encounter clients that are grumpy, demanding, and afraid of you ripping them off. The key is to have a POSITIVE ATTITUDE and don't take their bad attitude personally. Don't let the client's negativity cause you to reflect negativity back toward them. Understand in advance that if you can find a way to connect with the client and lower their defensiveness and fear you will most likely make a friend that will become a repeat client!

I hope in this first chapter that you have learned that by maintaining a positive attitude you will be able to overcome gut-punching adversity, make people laugh, win friends and earn long term repeat clients. Yes, I mentioned repeat clients again! In addition, from my personal experience, having a positive attitude makes everything in life better. Life can and will kick you in the teeth and car sales is a great example, however it is up to you to decide if you want to be positive or negative. If you decide to be positive you and your clients will be happier, and life will be good.

Now that I've given you some information on how I feel about attitude I will focus on product knowledge in the next chapter.

Chapter 2: Know Your Product

Early in my career the dealership I work for owned a new car franchise that were sort of unique cars – known as the "anti-status, status symbol" for the independent minded, scholarly, technical type clients who liked to stand apart from the crowd a bit. Many times, these clients would come into the showroom knowing more about the vehicles than I did. I had one gentleman visit one day and test drive a sedan made by this manufacturer and he ended up purchasing and taking delivery of the vehicle that day. Everything seemed to go very smooth and I felt like he and I got along well, and he liked me and the car. I thought he left a happy client. Well, at that time, our dealership owner sent a customer satisfaction survey to every customer that purchased a car and he read every one of them that was returned. Approximately one week after the deal my manager called me into his office and informed me that the owner of our dealership contacted him to inform him of a negative survey received from one of my customers. It turns out the customer had asked me if the exhaust system was made of stainless steel and I had replied that I did not know so he complained that his salesman's product knowledge was poor, and we should know everything about the car. The customer was right. As a car salesperson you should know every single detail of the product you're selling. For an uneducated slouch like me it's difficult to know everything about every vehicle and most automotive salespeople are worse than me, however I make it a point to work hard at studying my product and learn as much as I can about it. It's not as crucial in today's world thanks to internet voice searches you could do on your smart phone, because most answers for any question you could think of could be answered quickly by asking your smart phone. With that said, the more you study your product and the more you know about it determines how quickly you can provide answers to your customers. If you're able to provide accurate answers quickly to your clients without searching the internet you will have more credibility and be more professional than your competition.

I learned a valuable lesson from that client who bought the quirky car and I took it to heart because I was embarrassed that the owner received a bad survey from one of my clients. At the time I was very new in the car business – a "green pea" as rookie salespeople are often referred to by veteran salespeople and managers. The green pea term still doesn't make sense to me since I think all peas are green regardless of their age, aren't they? As a green pea I still felt like I was on double secret probation and didn't want any more negative customer satisfaction surveys, so I decided to show up one hour early every workday and spend that time learning my product. I would retrieve an owner's manual for a specific model, grab the key to an in-stock unit and sit in the car with the manual to learn what every single button was for and practice using them. By learning and practicing every function of the vehicle you will be able to confidently demonstrate the functionality of the vehicle to your clients and "W.O.W." them, rather than stumble and appear to be unprofessional and unprepared. By the way, the acronym "W.O.W." stands for "Wouldn't Own Without!" While you are learning your product, you need to pay attention to "W.O.W." factors your product offers and make sure you demonstrate these options to your prospective clients during your walk around and demonstration drive. Clients would much rather purchase from a salesperson who knows their stuff vs a salesperson that doesn't. As I believe I mentioned earlier in the book, a vehicle purchase is typically the second largest purchase people make during their life after their home so they prefer to deal with an expert and many times will pay more for excellent, knowledgeable service.

One prime example of a "W.O.W." factor I demonstrate is the remote start option. Most new and pre-owned models I sell have remote start as a factory option included and that is a huge advantage my product has over most of the makes and models I'm competing against. As I'm walking my clients to the vehicle we have selected to test drive, I begin to explain the remote start option. Some of my clients will immediately let me know they already have it and are familiar with its capabilities. Other clients that have it on their old vehicle didn't even know they had it and say – "Wow, I sure would like to have that for these cold winter days!" When I let them know they've had it, but it wasn't explained to them I instantly build credibility while the salesperson they purchased from last time loses credibility. It's not so much that you're steeling the business away from the last salesperson because chances are slim that salesperson would be there anyway the next time the client went back. However, the client will be far more likely to come back and see me for their next vehicle and become part of my repeat client base. At this point, I mention that the system is called "adaptive remote start" and that it will not only warm your vehicle in winter, it will also cool it down in summer! Not only that, it will accordingly turn on your heated or cooled seats! Next, I pull my phone out of my pocket and open the manufacturer's mobile app and show them how they could start their vehicle from their phone. "Wow" is what I hear most of the time. My point in rambling about the remote start option is that if you know your advantages you need to demonstrate those advantages. Even if the feature is one that your competitors have but it is a W.O.W. factor you still want to demonstrate that feature. Many times, I see salespeople just make a copy of the client's driver's license and send the client out on their own to test drive the car. This is a big mistake and I'll elaborate more on the demonstration drive later.

Another "W.O.W." feature is the voice command system that is part of the infotainment system. What is an infotainment system? I explain it as a tablet built into your dash and clients reply – "Wow!" Then I press the voice command button on the steering wheel and say the name of a radio station. The radio changes to that station and I say to my client – "See, it even understands my Wisconsin accent" and they always laugh at that line, unless they're from Minnesota, Canada or the upper peninsula of Michigan! Notice how I'm throwing in some humor right there at that moment? Remember me writing about well-timed humor? I didn't even know I had an accent until I moved to Illinois at 34 years old and many of my clients kept asking me – "Are you from Minnesota, Wisconsin, Canada or the U.P.?" So, I figured why not roll with it and make it part of my show. That's how I view the entire sales process with clients – putting on a show. The more you know your product, it's capabilities and advantages the more confident you will be with your show.

Another great way to know your product is by taking advantage of all the training resources available from the manufacturer. I've been selling the same brand at the same dealership my entire career, so their system is all I know, however their online training program is excellent. They also provide in showroom training via a third-party contract company that sends a trainer to the dealership to train salespeople on new technology, new features, functionality of safety features and of what features customers are reporting they are dissatisfied with. I always pay close attention to the training, especially the feature's customers are dissatisfied with because by mastering those features, I'm able to confidently demonstrate those features to my clients and train my clients on how to use them with confidence. That makes for a completely satisfied client and completely satisfied clients are far more likely to become, you guessed it, repeat clients!

From my experience, the most common features customers are dissatisfied with are Bluetooth, seat memory, climate controls and navigation. These are simple features to operate although many times there are simple little tips and tricks that if not explained can make the client frustrated and dissatisfied. For example, the current "infotainment system" most of my brand's models are equipped with have a touch screen volume control. This system was negatively reviewed by more than one of the car critics of the big magazines because of how difficult it was to operate. The fact of the matter is that it is not difficult to operate at all once someone is shown how to do it properly. I show my clients that by placing their finger right on the faceplate where it says "volume" and simply sliding their finger left or right from that center position, it is an easy adjustment. I can almost guarantee those who wrote those critical words weren't smart enough to figure it out on their own, so they slammed it. Once I show clients how to properly perform the operation (which I have made part of my test drive demonstration and delivery) they see how easy it is and it is a benefit, not a source of dissatisfaction. I guess the professional car critics couldn't figure out the volume controls on the steering wheel either. Or they just neglected to mention it because that would detract from their negative review.

For those features that are the biggest cause of customer dissatisfaction, I work extra hard at ensuring my clients have a complete understanding. In one of my part-time jobs while I was going to drafting school, I worked for a chain restaurant and they had a three-step training method that is based on the theory that the average person will remember something long term if they read it or do it three times. The training method is: 1. Trainer says, trainer does. 2. Trainer says, trainee does. 3. Trainee says, trainee does. I don't follow that method exactly however I do make sure I explain it, show it, and then have my clients do it themselves so I know they have it figured out. I've found this method to work well when training my clients on the operation of the features of their vehicle, even before they've made the purchase! Why do I do this? Because I know most of my competition isn't doing this and it shows the client that I care about their experience. I know for a fact most automotive salespeople don't demonstrate the features or train their clients because I witness it every day. Many salespeople don't even go on the test drive with their clients and what they don't realize is that they are missing huge, critical steps to a more successful outcome. You might be asking – Why wouldn't they do that? I believe the answer is fear. They are afraid because they haven't taken the time to learn the features themselves, so they don't have the confidence to demonstrate the features. They're afraid they will make a mistake or stumble and embarrass themselves. I believe this is true because it is how I felt when I started in the business, before the quirky car customer wrote the letter to the owner and I decided to learn my product. Once I learned my product inside and out, I had the confidence to properly demonstrate the vehicles to my clients and train them on how to properly operate the vehicle and its features.

Now I will elaborate a bit on online training. I view online training as a tremendous resource to provide me with the tools and knowledge I need to be a successful, professional, automotive sales consultant. It is not difficult to complete, however I feel the more time I put into it and focus on completely understanding the concepts, the more successful I will be. It provides courses on everything from how to appropriately address internet leads, phone etiquette, welcoming a client when they visit the dealership, how to provide an exceptional experience to your clients during their visit, very specific product knowledge for every model we offer, competitive product knowledge of the vehicles we compete against, how to understand vehicle leasing, and even how to protect the dealership from cybersecurity threats. I know many other salespeople who complete the training however they breeze through it without taking extra time to fully grasp it and in my opinion, they are only shortcutting their ability to be more successful. It requires work to fully understand the training and most sales consultants simply don't want to put forth the effort needed to take full advantage of the training provided.

To me, car sales is easy relative to many other jobs because I worked some tough jobs as a kid and when I was a young man – working on a poultry farm catching chickens and shoveling chicken manure, washing dishes in a restaurant, assembly jobs in factories and working in the chemical factory. With that said, you need to be able to deal with difficult personalities of customers, rejection, make a lot of phone calls, send a lot of emails, text messages, self-marketing and training. You must be committed to excellence and what it takes to be excellent. The online training is also a requirement to be eligible for the manufacturer sales bonus program however even if there were no financial benefit such as the bonus program, why wouldn't you want to take advantage of all the training available to you? It's just common sense to me that the more knowledge you have of your products features, the better suited and more comfortable you will be demonstrating those features and therefore, more likely to get the sale and commission. If you are feeling comfortable with your product, you will feel comfortable with your clients and you will have confidence. Your clients will feel like they are dealing with an expert. It took me a long time to get comfortable demonstrating a car to a prospective client. It wasn't a natural thing for me, so I had to work at it to get good at it. There's that four-letter word again – work!

When I would grab an owner's manual, key and go sit in the new cars to learn the features I would also pretend I was "delivering" the vehicle to client who had just purchased it. You might ask, why is someone buying a car referred to as "taking delivery?" Well, per Wikipedia one of the definitions of the phrase "take delivery of" means "receive (something purchased.") It doesn't always mean delivering something to someone like a pizza is delivered. As I mentioned, I've only sold cars for one manufacturer however I do know, from speaking with sales consultants from other manufacturers, that other manufacturers also require many hours of continuous online training. The key is to really work hard on fully understanding the training and then implementing the training and follow the process. Knowledge is worthless until it is applied knowledge.

I have taken the approach since I began my career to soak up as much training as possible and it has paid off. I continue to soak up as much training as possible because vehicle technology is consistently changing, usually improving. If you are on top of your product and aware of new technology or safety features, then you will have a huge advantage over your competition. For instance, let's say I'm demonstrating a vehicle to a prospective client and they have mentioned how important safety features are to them. Once they've told me safety is their primary concern, I make sure I let them know about the Lane Departure Warning, Rear Cross Traffic Alert, Forward Collision Alert, Forward Automatic Braking, Auto Dry Disc Brakes with ABS, all included for $54,055. Now, let's say the same client goes to look at a competitive model and the client asks the sales consultant (your competition) if the vehicle they are demonstrating has all the same features. If your competition is not as knowledgeable as you were during your description of your products safety features, they will be less confident. Since they're less confident they will stumble, make stuff up, avoid answering direct questions from the customer and therefore, you will be much more credible. Be the expert and customers will come back to you and buy your product because of you! It doesn't happen every time because there are times when a client simply likes your competition's product better from a style or technology standpoint and they will buy it from an unknowledgeable salesperson anyway. Personally though, I have a massive client base of clients who only buy from me and don't even look at other brands. I've also had many clients tell me that even though they test drove competitive models and liked the competitive model better than the model we had to offer, they still came back to me due to the level of service and product knowledge I provide. I'm also told often by new prospects how much better their experience was with me vs the other three or four dealers they visited and part of that is due to knowing my product. My rugged good looks, charming personality and splendid sense of humor don't hurt either, LOL! I'm no swell looker however I am charming and funny so that makes up for my lack of natural beauty. By rugged good looks, I do mean rugged.

The other aspect of product knowledge that is critical to my success selling cars is knowing how to properly respond to a question when I don't know the answer. Truth reigns supreme in these situations. As I mentioned earlier, I often see other salespeople provide wrong answers to customers. I'm not sure why they do it. It might be because they want to look like the expert and it's easier to make something up then look it up or spend time in advance learning the product. Or, maybe they just don't remember accurately what the true answers are and think they are providing the correct answer. I'm just speculating however I think those are two main reasons why but what really matters here is that when you provide false information the odds are good that you will lose a client because of it. If you don't know the correct answer asked of you by a client, then let them know that you will find the correct answer for them. In these times we're living in right now, it's usually as simple as utilizing internet search tools. My main go-to resource for product knowledge is my manufacturers Web site that provides almost every bit of information I need to answer any questions regarding available colors, trim levels, and specifications. I prefer to utilize resources from the manufacturer whenever possible because even though internet search tools are continually improving at providing accurate information, there is still a chance you could be provided with incorrect information if you don't choose a link from a credible source.

The main take away you need from me explaining the importance of providing correct answers is that if you don't provide correct answers, you will lose your credibility, lose your client's trust and ultimately, lose the car deal. Most prospective clients do many hours of online research before visiting a dealership so many of them know as much or more about the vehicle than the salespeople trying to sell them the vehicle. Therefore, it is probable that they will know when the salesperson is bullshitting them. I have done training of other salespeople for past managers I've had and one the most important things I stressed to the trainee's is – DON'T BULLSHIT THE CUSTOMER! I always ask them if they are offended by the word "bullshit" first, and if so, I use the term "lie."

So hopefully you get the idea of how knowing your product, knowing your competitive advantages, practicing your products "wouldn't own without" or "W.O.W." factors and knowing how to smoothly and professionally demonstrate those advantages and features will be beneficial to your success selling cars. And I'll say it again - earn repeat clients!

Chapter 3: Make it Happen

Now that I've explained how I maintain a positive attitude and how important product knowledge is I'm going to share with you how I "make it happen!" The phrase "make it happen" is as simple as that, however another way I think of it is "action creates action." Breaking it down further, to me it means you must put in the work necessary to create positive results by being ambitious, creative and taking extra action to generate car sales. This might seem obvious to some people however during my career selling cars, I've noticed most of my peers do not put forth any extra effort to generate business. Most wait for the business to come to them. Waiting for the business is just fine if you're happy earning the average car salesperson income, however if you want to earn twice as much as the average car salesperson (as I have done for 9 years in a row) then you need to take extra action. Go beyond what is expected of you by your manager, GM and owner. The car salespeople that put forth extra effort are the ones that reap the rewards of mores sales and more income because they "make it happen!"

When I started in the car business, I hadn't even fully moved to Illinois yet from WI and was "shacking up" (as my Dad Carl used to say) with my girlfriend at the time who shortly after that became my wife. Since I was new to the area I was working in, I had no family or friends living close by to sell cars to, which in my opinion are the first people you should network with once you become a car sales consultant. Immediately upon starting my career I tried to let everyone I knew know that I was now a car salesman, but not all of them because in my case it didn't produce a lot of sales because the dealership was a 2.5-hour drive from my home town where I spent the first 34 years of my life living within 30 miles of its location.

One thing I've observed is that people like to purchase a vehicle as close to where they live as possible although this is changing a little. I have seen more and more clients fly in from all parts of the US to buy cars. If you have the vehicle they want, they will travel for it or have it shipped to them. With that said, most people still like to buy their car close to where they live so if you happen to land your first car sales job close to where you have a lot of friends, family and acquaintances then it will be an advantage for you, provided you reach out to them and let them know you could assist them with their next car. Whether you land your first car sales job close to your home town or not, get the word out that you are a car sales consultant to every single family member, friend, acquaintance, former co-worker and enemy that you know and I'm confident you will generate some car sales from those people as well as people they know.

Early on especially, however throughout your career, referrals will be a large percentage of your business if you do things the right way. By doing "things the right way" I mean treating your clients openly, honestly, ethically, as well as everything else I write about in this book. This is why starting to develop your "book of business" by reaching out to every family member, friend, and acquaintance is the best way to start because these contacts already know what a great person you are, they know you have integrity and you have earned their trust already. If they don't like you or trust you then for obvious reasons, you probably don't want to ask them for their vehicle business or referrals. Or your enemies. I was joking a bit by mentioning enemies in the previous paragraph. The point here is that the people you know will be more likely to buy a car from you and refer their friends and family to you – if you ask for the referral! That's right, you need to ask for referrals. Asking for referrals is crucial because if you do ask then the odds of your friends, family, acquaintances, prospects and previous clients thinking about you while discussing vehicles with their contacts increases significantly.

The main point of these first few paragraphs is that the people you already know will be your best first contacts in your client base you will need to develop. The biggest lesson is that if you don't reach out to these people and let them know you are there to assist them with their next vehicle you will end up finding out that they bought a new car somewhere else when you could have sold it to them! You will then feel foolish that you didn't let them know you are a car salesperson and fear that they were not taken care of as well as you would have taken care of them. I know because I've had it happen. One time I was visiting with a relative at a family gathering and they told me how they bought a car somewhere else because they didn't know I was a car salesman. It will happen and when it does it is very important to not take it personally. It's part of the business and you don't earn every "deal", so you have to "deal" with it and don't upset yourself over it. Move on to the next potential client with a smile on your face knowing there are millions of other potential sales out there waiting for you!

In today's world of 2019 if I was just starting my car sales career the no-brainer to "make it happen" would be to generate business via social media. I started a social media page last year however I haven't put much effort into it because I'm too busy already assisting my repeat clients and new clients generated from our business development center as well as the occasional "walk in client." I'm going to continue to mention repeat clients throughout this book because that is my "bread and butter" and it's a beautiful thing. If you are just starting and don't have your client base of loyal customers already established, social media is where it's at. I wish social media would have been mainstream when I started selling cars because I don't see any better way to generate car sales at this point in history.

Another analogy I picked up along the way in my car sales career is that car sales is a lot like farming. You need to plant seeds to produce a bountiful harvest. The beauty of car sales is that you never know when the seeds will sprout, flower, and convert to produce. It's not like you plant them in the spring and harvest them in the fall because every client buying cycle is different. Real farming is more predictable although my cousin Mark who is a dairy farmer would probably disagree. Real farmers have their challenges with mother nature affecting how much hay and corn they harvest. His milk production is much more predictable though. The important point here is that if you plant the seeds now, sales will grow from them and you will "make it happen!"

One somewhat predictable cycle in car sales is new car leases. A large portion of my business are clients who lease a new car every two, three or four years so those clients are the best. The new car lease cycle is more consistent, sort of like milk production on the dairy farm however not as frequent (cousin Mark milks his cows twice per day.) None the less, it is a predictable sales cycle. Some clients prefer leasing because it gives them more flexibility with what brand they could drive so they can change brands easily however a high percentage of them return to lease the same brand repeatedly. Brand loyalty is common with people and cars. I have too many clients to count that return lease after lease. Much of their loyalty is also to me due to how I took care of them on the previous sale, providing them an attentive, knowledgeable luxury car buying experience and being there for them after the sale. Developing, maintaining and following up with your lease client portfolio is another great way to "make it happen!"

Another advantage of leasing is that the client is always driving a newer model vehicle with the latest styling, technology and safety features and their vehicle is typically covered by the original "bumper to bumper" warranty for the full term of the lease. Not to mention, they have a much lower payment for the same term vs a finance contract because they are only paying for the depreciation of the vehicle. Depreciation is the difference between the msrp of the new vehicle vs the residual value of the vehicle. The residual value is determined by the lender (lesser) and is the value they predict the vehicle will be worth at the end of the lease term. In summary, leasing is more like dairy farming because it is more predictable than sales that are cash or finance contract purchases.

I have a whole chapter coming up on just follow up however even when I've lost track of clients in my customer relations management (CRM) tool they still ask for me when they come back because many of them say that I provided them with the best car buying experience they ever had. I recently even had a repeat client tell me that she test drove the competitive model to ours and liked it better than the model I had sold her for her last 4 leases, but she was going to lease another vehicle from me due to the level of service I provide. Provide your clients with the best car buying experience they have ever had, and you will "make it happen!"

Another analogy of car sales is that you could compare it to hunting. There are many hunting techniques for harvesting wild game and the same goes for selling cars. In many hunting situations you need to cover a lot of ground. You might cover that ground by all-terrain vehicle, by boat, by foot or even by airplane in far-away remote places like Alaska. In car sales, you need to cover a lot of ground by phone calls, text messages, email, and social media. You need to "make it happen" by covering a lot of territory in hunting and by covering a lot of potential clients in car sales. Patience is another key element to hunting that you also need to possess in car sales. You will not harvest game on every hunt. Sometimes the animals just don't cooperate and similarly, in car sales you won't close the deal with every potential client, so you need to be patient.

Fishing is another activity that is like selling cars. In fishing, you need to spend "time on the water" (TOTW.) In car sales, you need to spend "time on the lot" (TOTL.) If you're not on the water, you won't catch any fish and in car sales, if you're not on the lot, you won't sell many cars. I suppose you could sell cars from home or remotely via computer however you won't sell very many because even though consumers are buying vehicles sight unseen, remotely via the internet, most still do not buy until they have visited the dealership to see the vehicle first hand and test drive the vehicle. In fact, in many cases, clients that were so dead set on a specific model after conducting many hours of online research purchase something completely different once they test drive that specific model. They find out there is something they really don't like about it such as the leg room, the head room or the color doesn't look the same in person as it did on the internet. The more common reason clients change vehicle of interest is because they didn't realize the vehicle they came to see is missing one of their "must have" options. Sunroof, navigation, heated seats, heated steering wheel, and specific safety features are common options people forget to check for while doing their online research. This is another close analogy to fishing – you might find a nice fish on the sonar and the fish is looking at your bait but not biting so you must present a different bait. You must present a bait or lure the fish will want to eat, bite it, and then you set the hook and real 'em in! When fishing, the more casts of the lure or bait you make, the more fish you catch. In car sales, the more phone calls, text messages, emails and social media posts and advertisements, the more car sales you will close. There is an old saying in fishing – "the best lure is a wet one!" The analogy to car sales for this saying is that just like having your lure or bait in the water by utilizing your fishing pole, you need to utilize your phone and computer in car sales to make a lot of casts, therefore reeling in more car sales!

Another great way to "make it happen" is to spend time in the service drive of your dealership. The service drive is like a gold mine with lots of nuggets waiting to be mined. All you need to do is a little digging. By digging, I mean engaging the customers that are at your dealership having their car serviced. I've earned many sales and repeat clients in the service drive at my dealership by simply engaging people. For instance, there are many times when the service advisor/s are busy assisting service customers and there are one, two or three customers waiting for assistance. By simply greeting these people and offering them a beverage or snack while they're waiting, I've started conversations. I do my best not to get into long philosophical conversations because I need to maximize every minute of every day I'm at the dealership and making a conversation too long is inefficient. Once I break the ice by offering a beverage or snack, I will ask them point blank – "Would you be interested in a no obligation appraisal of your current vehicle?" Then, without pausing, I will tell them – "We need used vehicles for our used car inventory and my used car manager is paying top dollar for them." I've been selling cars for many years and there has never been a time when my used car manager wasn't looking to purchase used cars for inventory. Many times, the client will agree, and they will tell you that they would like to look at the new models while the appraisal is being completed. Many times, they will tell me "no thanks" and let me know they are happy with the vehicle they have. If they tell me no then I simply hand them a business card and let them know I'm there for them if they ever need anything down the road. I'm not pushy because no one likes to be pressured into doing something they don't want to do. Even though I didn't get a deal at that moment, many clients remember me when they are ready for a car since I made them feel welcome and gave them the feeling that they will be treated well when they are ready to buy another vehicle.

A lot of times service clients are there for simple reasons like their tire pressure is low or they have an issue with their Bluetooth phone connection, and I solve their problem for them without service getting involved. Many times, I've jumped into service and adjusted tire pressure for clients or solved their Bluetooth issue or assisted them with resetting their seat memory and got them on their way quickly. Time is very important to people so if you can save them a little time, they greatly appreciate it and many of those clients I've assisted in the service drive have returned later and purchased a vehicle from me.

Another advantage of assisting clients in the service drive is that your service advisors will appreciate the assistance and when they have a client that needs or wants a new vehicle, they will refer those clients to you because you were helpful to them. That's a great way to "make it happen!" I make it a point to let my service advisors know I'm there to assist them if any of their clients require assistance with Bluetooth pairing for their phones, personalization issues with their comfort and convenience features or operational questions for their infotainment system (radio/nav/apps.) It's another planted seed that will produce some produce in the future.

One thing I did when I started in the business to make it happen was partnering up with credit unions and banks that offer vehicle lending options. I phoned a bunch of local banks and credit unions and asked them for the person in charge of vehicle lending. I let them know I was a car salesman and asked them if they would be willing to allow me to post a flyer in their lobby letting their clients know I was a trusted partner of the bank or credit union. The dealership I work for is a well-known dealership with a great reputation, so it was a no-brainer for them to work with me. This was a great way to generate business and a couple of lenders I worked with put my flyer in their monthly newsletter. I made personal visits to the banks and credit unions so the contact there could put a face to my name, and I would offer to take them out to lunch to build a relationship and it worked well. I picked up one, two and many times, three or more extra deals per month with this strategy. These days, you probably wouldn't even have to do the personal visit because the world is so electronically driven. You could video chat from your phone with your bank and credit union contacts and design your own flyer or have a graphic designer design one for you and send it via email. The banks and credit unions could then post it in their e-newsletters, Web sites, and on their printed promotional products. Yes, printed products do still exist and are effective, otherwise they would not still exist. Also, even more powerful than flyers, e-newsletters and Web sites, I'm sure social media is in play with banks and credit unions who finance vehicles so I'm sure these lenders could share your social media page too by promoting your partnership on their social media.

As I mentioned earlier in the book, there are so many cars in America and most adults own one. When I internet searched working age population in the U.S. I found out that in 2010 there were 194.3 million people working age from 18-64 and if you add the people over 64 and under 18 that own cars you're talking about a massive number of potential clients! So the main point I've tried to make in this chapter is you need to "make it happen" by reaching as many of these people as possible because there is strength in numbers and the more people you reach, the more vehicles you will sell. I know there are many other ways to generate car sales however the methods above are what got me to the point of having a tremendous repeat client base that returns again and again for their vehicle needs. Until you've established your repeat client base you need to go out and find the business. You will always need to continue to gain new clients because every client you sell won't return so you need to continue farming, hunting and fishing throughout your career. The longer you stay in one place and take care of and maintain contact with your previous clients though, the less you will have to generate new business however it is always part of my focus. Finally setting up a social media page is the current example of what I'm doing to generate new business. Fortunately, as of late, I've been too busy selling cars to work on my social media page however my goal is to start utilizing that tool more often to "gain and retain" clients and "MAKE IT HAPPEN!"

Chapter 4: Road to the Sale

In car sales, there is a sales process called the "road to the sale." It's a defined step by step sales process that my dealership has their sales consultants utilize to assist clients with their vehicle purchase. The road to the sale was in play when I started selling cars and I'm sure it was around long before I became involved in the car world. I have seen several variations over the years presented by different training organizations and managers however the road to the sale that I follow is very similar, if not the same, as the one I learned when I started my career. I will dive into it here for you and whether you are considering car sales as a career, just started selling cars, or already have been in the car sales business, hopefully you will pick up a tip or two that have been successful for me.

One observation I have, looking back on my entire career, is that the car business is constantly changing. Managers come and go, other salespeople come and go, Customer Relations Management (CRM) tools change, different training companies are in and out, the vehicles themselves change, and customers change. I've found that there is always some change happening that I must adapt to. Being able to adapt has been something I've been pretty good at, so I feel that is one of the reasons for my longevity at one dealership. Working at only one dealership is one constant I've had, and the other constant is the road to the sale. The main idea of the road to the sale is the same as when I started my career although there are two main steps that have evolved and I will elaborate on those in the paragraphs that follow, as I break down each step in more detail.

Here are the main steps in my road to the sale:

1. Meet and Greet

2. Consultation

3. Appraisal/Walk Around

4. Test Drive

5. Trial Close

6. Negotiation/Proposal

7. Close

8. Follow Up

The first step in the road to the sale is the meet and greet. So, I've made it happen, I've set my appointment, confirmed the appointment and I'm anxiously awaiting the arrival of my prospective client and ready for the meet and greet! I wrote about first impression earlier in the book so there will probably be a lot of duality in the following comments however anything repeated about first impression during the meet in greet is worth re-mentioning. When my clients arrive at the dealership, whether I greet them at the showroom door or one of my associates greets them and brings them to me, I go into "the happy zone." I make a very conscious effort to be happy and smile. Even if I'm in a bad mood, I know that I must flip the switch to happy mode, so I make a great first impression with my prospect.

Most days, when I'm working the car lot, I'm in a good mood because I see the car business as a great opportunity. I see it as my own business with no overhead costs. Other than my transportation expenses to and from the dealership and my wardrobe, I have no overhead costs. The inventory is acquired and managed by the dealership, they pay for my phone, my computer, internet, desk, showroom, marketing and even provide lunch on Saturdays! In addition, I have the benefits of a full-time employee with a 401k retirement plan, health insurance, and life insurance. All I need to do is show up and work hard to sell a car. I got a little off topic because what I started to write about in this paragraph is being in a good mood. I feel being in a good mood is critical to my success because my clients feel the good mood vibes I'm projecting, and it makes them feel good too. If the client feels good, they will be more likely to like you. If they like you, they will be more likely to buy from you. If they really like you, they will become repeat clients. If I'm not in a good mood, then I utilize the techniques I mentioned earlier in the book to change my mood. I won't go into as much detail as I did earlier however "the old buddy" trick works for me and you will need to find out what works for you.

Once I have myself in "the happy zone" and I approach the client I use two different greetings. The first one is for clients I haven't met yet and goes like this – "Welcome to (the name of my dealership), how could I assist you?" Most often, the client tells me that they are there to see a specific vehicle, they have an appointment with another salesperson, they have a service appointment or they're "just looking." The other greeting I utilize is "welcome back!" If I have a repeat client coming in (which I do most days) my greeting to them is always a huge smile, extended hand to shake and I say enthusiastically – "Welcome back!" We had a service advisor named Mondo who I worked with when I started in the business and that was his greeting, even to fellow employees. When he said it to me, it made me feel great, so I stole it from Mondo and have used it ever since. I'll even say it sometimes if I never met the prospect because I think it makes them feel like they should know me, and they feel recognized. One thing I learned somewhere along the way is that every human enjoys and greatly appreciates being recognized. They also enjoy the sound of their own name so any time I can address them by name, I do.

Getting back to why the prospect is at your dealership, if the prospect tells you they are there to see a specific salesperson, manager, or they are looking for service then I always walk them to whoever it is they came to see. Even though the prospect isn't there to see me, there is a chance for me to earn their business by walking them to their contact as opposed to just pointing and telling them where to go. You might be asking – "How could that happen?" Well, what if you walk the client down to the other salesperson and they're not there or they are too busy to assist the client? The other salesperson might ask you to assist the client and split the deal with you. A half deal is better than no deal, I always say, however I'm not a big fan of split deals. I would rather help my fellow salesperson out and then they will be obligated to help me when I need it. If the prospect has arrived and asked to see a manager and I walk them to the manager, there is high probability that manager will ask me to assist the prospect if the prospect is there to see a car. One big mistake is to introduce the client to the manager and walk away. I always hang out for a while until I know if the manager is going to request my assistance or not and many times they do, and I get a sale out of it. If the prospect is visiting to see a service manager or service advisor, I will strike up a conversation as I'm walking the guest to them and try to make a favorable impression on the guest so the next time they need a different vehicle they remember me. I've sold many cars months and even years after assisting a client by simply walking them to a fellow employee they've arrived to see so this is another simple detail that has added sales and repeat clients to my client portfolio throughout my career.

Another very important part of the meet and greet is establishing rapport. A great way to do this is to comment on any logos your prospect might have on their clothing or hat. If I know the logo and I have some bit of knowledge about it, then I will usually ask the prospect their thoughts. For instance, the prospect is wearing a Chicago Bears hat and I know the Bears lost their previous game, I will tell them I'm sorry for their loss. If they're wearing golf gear, then I'll ask them "how's your golf game?" Most men and women golfers love to talk about their game, good or bad. If you're a golfer and can speak a little golf lingo with them that's a great way to establish common ground. Even if you're not a golfer but have tried it and couldn't play very well, that's a great opportunity to make the prospect feel good by complimenting them and letting them know how admirable you are of them for being able to play the game. Very competitive golfers might not want to talk about their game if they've been playing badly of late. If that's that case, move on to a different topic. If the client is wearing something related to fishing and they fish themselves, it's game over with me. Since I used to do a lot of fishing, when I get a chance to talk about it, I'm genuinely super excited and super happy so that brings the prospect up another level of happy too. Another great way to establish rapport is to compliment the prospect on their shoes. Example: I own a pair of brand name boat shoes and a lot of my prospects and clients wear the same brand so I will say – "Nice pair of (insert brand name here) you're wearing, aren't they great?" They now know that you have worn them too, so you have established common ground and therefore, rapport. Boom! If your prospect is wearing a logo that you are not familiar with, or an article of clothing you admire but don't recognize, then a great way to make them feel good is to ask them what it is. Simple as – "What does the logo on your hat represent?" Or – "I really like your shoes." These simple things show the prospect or client that you are genuinely interested in them and once again, they will feel good. These techniques don't always work, (remember me talking about the "ten percenters?") however they work at least 90% of the time, I'm guessing 99% of the time for me. I think I have a very high level of success with this because I am genuinely interested in other people, what they do, and what they enjoy. When the client feels you are sincere, they like you better and you know what that means when they like you better – more likely to buy from you and more likely to become a repeat client!

The next thing I do in the meet and greet is offer my prospect or client a beverage or snack. It's just a nice, simple gesture that makes them feel welcome. The dealership I work for provides beverages and snacks, as I believe most dealerships do, however if yours doesn't, I would recommend having your own stash to offer. If the client declines my offer, I still bring them water and let them know it's there for them, just in case they need to wet their whistle. If the prospect or client would like a beverage or snack, I will immediately let them know I'm going to get it for them and will be right back. "Please excuse me while I get that coffee for you." I try to act like the wait staff at a high-end restaurant so the prospect feels special, just as they would sitting down to order a $100 tomahawk ribeye steak.

Once you have greeted your client, exchanged a couple of comments to establish rapport and offered a beverage, the next step is inviting them to your desk for the consultation step in the road to the sale. After I have greeted my clients with enthusiasm and set them up with a beverage and/or snack, I turn toward my desk and waive the prospect toward it, and I say – "please follow me." Most clients will follow me right over but not all of them. If the client prefers to look around the showroom first and is there just to look, that's ok. There are still some prospects that come into the showroom just to look and are not ready for a test drive, so they won't follow me to my desk. When this happens, I just do the consultation while walking with them. In either case, whether at the desk, or walking with the client around the showroom or on the lot, the consultation is the piece of the road to the sale that I utilize to find out as much as I can about the client and what they're trying to accomplish.

Through the years, the dealership I work for has had several different consultation forms they require salespeople to complete to gather key information that will have a role to play in the sale. These forms usually start with questions regarding the current vehicle the prospect is looking to replace or already have replaced. The key questions I ask are: What make and model is it? I ask because when I go out with the client to conduct the appraisal, I will know what I'm looking for. Also, once I know what vehicle the prospect currently or recently has driven it will also lead me to questions for them such as: What do they use the vehicle for? This question could be valuable if your prospect is having difficulty choosing what type of vehicle they would like next. For instance, if a father of three kids with car seats who drops those kiddos off at school every day came in to see an SUV and then gets distracted and wants to test drive a sporty two door coupe, you may need to remind him that the two door coupe will not accommodate his car seats and refocus his attention to the SUV. Personal vehicles are an emotional purchase and sometimes clients aren't thinking clearly so I see it as my obligation as their sales consultant to assist them with maintaining focus on what's best for them. If they insist on changing direction with their vehicle focus then I don't talk them out of it, I only make suggestions. Is it leased, financed or paid for? If leased or financed, what is the monthly payment? What is your monthly payment goal or total budget for the new or used vehicle your considering as a replacement? These questions are important because the client may want to lower their monthly payment due to other new expenses, like college tuition or medical bills or they have a new job earning less money. They may have just started a new job with a higher salary or received a large bonus so they would like to spend a little more on an upgraded model. Many clients want to keep their payment the same because nothing has changed in their life and they're comfortable with their current situation.

Once I know what my prospect is trying to accomplish with their budget, I have a couple of simple guestimate techniques I utilize to target the right vehicle for them. If they have a specific amount of cash to spend and would like to pay one lump sum for the vehicle then that's obvious, I show them what we have to offer in their price range. If they would like to be at a specific payment for a finance contract the simple guestimate math that is fairly accurate is this: Take the first two digits of the price of the vehicle, I'll use $10,000 as an example, and multiply by two – 10 x 2 = 20, add a 0 to the 20 and your approximate 60 month finance payment would be $200 per month with $0 down, "assuming top tier credit rating." So, for a $20,000 car the 60-month payment would be approximately $400 per month, a $25,000 car = $500 per month and so on. Utilizing this technique will prevent you from wasting time showing a prospect a $60,000 car when they want their monthly payment to be $500 per month with $0 down. When they tell me they would like to test drive the $60,000 vehicle I politely inform them that the payment would be approximately $1,200 per month, not their desired $500 payment. I will usually phrase it like this: "Are you prepared and willing to increase your vehicle budget by that amount?" Most will reply no however sometimes they will say yes, so I react accordingly.

Now let's say the prospect would like to lease and they would like to take advantage of the manufacturer lease advertisement of $349 with $4,000 down plus taxes on a $45,000 msrp vehicle however they must have the heated seats, heated steering wheel, sun roof, imbedded navigation and AWD so the msrp of the vehicle they really want is $55,000. The simple guestimate on lease payments is for every $1,000 in msrp of the vehicle that will impact the payment approximately $20 per month. Therefore, if you have a $10,000 difference in msrp the payment for the $55k vehicle will be approximately $200 higher per month. I always explain this math to my prospects and ask them what is more important, the payment or the additional options?

With that said, don't be afraid to show them what you have in stock that might be higher or lower than their budget because many times people end up spending more or less than they planned on, depending on what their "hot button" might be. The "hot button" is a feature, color, engine choice, model, seating configuration, or anything that the prospect must have in their new vehicle. For instance, a client would like to take advantage of the manufacturers lease special of $349 per month with $4,000 down however that special is on a standard model with no heated seats, no heated steering wheel and no driver awareness package. Once I inform them the standard model doesn't have those features, I ask if they are willing to pay more for those features. Some reply no, some reply yes, so now the prospect and I can effectively work together to select the right vehicle for them. Assisting prospects with deciphering these situations builds value in me as their sales consultant as well and the more valuable I become to the prospect, the more they will appreciate me and the more likely they will buy from me and become repeat clients.

Now that I just wrote a bit about the prospect consultation, I can tell you that more and more often the consultation is done before the client arrives at the dealership. In fact, many prospects complete the entire consultation themselves before they contact a dealership for the first time and very often, they contact the dealership that has the vehicle they have targeted. With consumers able to see every single available vehicle in the Country from their phone and the fact that there is so much information online now, it has had an incredible impact on exposure to the inventory you are selling as well as the amount of research prospects are able to do from their pc, phone or tablet. This has also made the car sales consultant profession easier regarding clients being far more dialed in on the vehicle they would like before visiting the dealership. The days of test driving 4 or 5 cars to select the right one for the client are extremely rare, if not gone for good. I can't remember the last time I test drove more than two vehicles with a client and typically I only do one test drive with my prospects. Especially if I've done a thorough consultation!

The next step in the road to the sale is the appraisal/walk around. If the prospect has a vehicle they would like to trade in, as soon as I've completed my consultation, I ask the prospect to show me their trade vehicle. Now I will do a walk around of their vehicle. A walk around consists of exactly that – walking around the vehicle. What I look to accomplish while walking around their vehicle is to look for any excess wear and tear (dings, dents, scratches, excess tire wear and interior condition) as well as how their current vehicle is equipped or what items are in or on their trade. If I notice any excess wear and tear, I don't mention it although I will touch it with my finger just to let the prospect know that I have noticed it. The prospect will usually tell you what caused the damage or wear, and this assists them in realizing their trade may not be as nice as they described to you during the consultation and therefore, not as valuable as they thought it might be. Next, I let the prospect know that part of our trade appraisal process is to take a brief test drive around the block. I drive their car and check for any potential issues such as warning lights, abnormal engine noise, brake noise and brake pulsation, suspension issues and any other mechanical issues. Here again, if there are any mechanical issues the client usually is aware of them however by you driving their vehicle with them, they now know that you are aware of the issues. They will again realize their vehicle may not be as valuable as the online appraisal tool they utilized to value it. If they selected "excellent condition" when they did their research, both of us now know that the vehicle is not in "excellent condition." If the vehicle is in perfect condition, then I will complement the prospect on the condition of their vehicle and let them know my used car manager would love to have it for our used car inventory. Vehicles in excellent condition will sell for more money and are easier to sell and require less reconditioning cost so of course any used car manager loves these types of trade vehicles and will allow a higher value for them to make a deal.

The next walk around will be on the vehicle my prospect is considering buying. Whether the client has selected the vehicle before arriving at the dealership or the prospect and I have selected the vehicle together during the consultation, a thorough walk around, and full test drive is something I do for every deal. It's crucial for several reasons. First, to make sure it is the right vehicle for the client – do they like the color? Is the equipment acceptable? Second, the test drive will assist the prospect with making sure they're comfortable in the vehicle ergonomically and visually. Third, the prospect will begin thinking about how the vehicle will fit into their life and this will assist them in determining if it is the right vehicle for them. Getting back to the walk around, the first thing I do is make sure I pull the vehicle up for the client and park it close to the showroom door in the guest parking for two reasons. First, the client doesn't have to walk around the lot with me to find the vehicle. Second, if the vehicle is dirty or out of gas, I'm able to quickly address those issues out of sight of the prospect. By not having any issues in front of the prospect my presentation will be more professional. If I know in advance what vehicle my client is coming to see, I always do my best to have the vehicle cleaned and gassed before they arrive at the dealership. If it's rainy or cold or snowing, I bring the vehicle into the shop for the walk around to provide the prospect an opportunity to see the vehicle in a comfortable setting. Just another small action that provides a much more pleasurable experience for the prospect vs. my competition that may have assisted them prior, or they might go visit next. If the previous or next salesperson the prospect worked with at a different dealership walks the prospect out to the car in the rain, cold or snow, hops in and says "let's go" and doesn't let them take their time looking around it's my opinion that the prospect is much more likely to buy from me because I made it a more pleasurable experience.

The first thing I do in my walk around is demo the remote vehicle starting system, if equipped. I wrote about it earlier in the book however it deserves further mention. Fortunately for the brand I sell, remote start is on almost every trim level of every model they offer and it's a huge advantage over most of our key competition. It's a definite "W.O.W" factor and I have found many times prospects are trading in a car with this feature and didn't even know they had it or didn't know how to use it. When that happens, it really shows the prospect that I'm an expert and who doesn't want to buy any product from an expert? This sentence is being written after a three day break from writing and what do you know, It happened again – A client came in at 10:00 (with very short notice) this week to take delivery of the exact same model they purchased previously from one of our other sales people who wasn't supposed to start his shift until noon. I jumped in to help the client on behalf of the other salesman and the client asked me – "Where's the car, I haven't even seen it yet." Having been just thrown into the situation I let her know I was glad to show it to her so I walked her out to the car and the first thing I did was stop about 10 feet from the vehicle, held the remote up to eye level of the guest, pressed and held the remote start button and started the car. Her eyes got wide and she said - "That's nice, I never had that before!" I said, "Well, you did in fact have it on your last vehicle and I'm sorry your previous salesperson didn't show you how to operate it." Letting the client know it wasn't their fault they didn't know about it and indirectly scolding the previous salesperson helps prevent the client from feeling stupid that they didn't know about it. Not only that, the salesman I was helping hadn't shown her the feature either so I made an impression on her and there's an excellent chance she will be back to see me when she needs to replace this lease. In addition, yesterday (one day after helping my associate with this client that didn't know about her remote start feature) I was right in the middle of selling a car and one of my other clients walked in unannounced two days earlier than our scheduled appointment. Since I had assisted my associate the day before, he jumped and in helped me with my unannounced guest. What goes around, comes around as they say so it paid off that I assisted the remote start client.

The next thing I do is walk around the vehicle pointing out the exterior features and, in my explanations, I make it a point to use the proper names of the features. For example, "This SUV is equipped with the 22" diameter 12 spoke high polished aluminum wheels." I just think it sounds better than – "This one's got 22's." Another example is "Galvano Satin chrome trim" rather than just saying "chrome." Instead of saying "here's a brown one" I will say "This one is the very elegant Bronze Dune Metallic." I am aware however, that the description of the option or color must be appropriate for the prospect so I'm trying to sell some biker dude, I'm not going to call it "elegant Bronze Dune Metallic," I'll refer to it as "kick-ass Bronze." Another one – "Front and rear ultrasonic parking assist sensors" as opposed to "it's got the beepers, so you don't hit anything." This is where knowing my product really helps me to project a far more professional image than most of my competition and all the time I spend studying my training materials and paying attention to our product trainer pays off. The next thing I will do is open the hood and trunk. I know the specs of the power train in case I'm asked but most times the clients know the engine specs already so I don't think it needs to be disclosed although I will mention the Direct Injection and Variable Valve Timing and let the prospect know that these are part of the reason the vehicle has over 300 hp with only 6 cylinders. Opening the hood also allows the prospect to see a brand-new shiny engine with no road grime like they may have seen when they refilled their windshield washer fluid reservoir last week. Seeing a nice, new shiny engine gets them thinking it sure would be nice to have a nice, new car with a shiny engine. At my dealership our detail department cleans the engine compartments on our used cars too so I will show my used car prospects under the hood as well, so they get a glimpse of a shiny clean engine vs their old grimy vehicle.

When showing the trunk or cargo area, it helps to know the cargo volume figure – "This vehicle has 18 cubic feet of trunk space, the largest of the full-size luxury sedan segment" as opposed to "you could fit two bodies in here." If the vehicle is equipped with a remotely powered lift gate, or better yet, the motion activated power lift gate this is a feature I will demonstrate every time – another "WOW" factor. If it's a crossover or sport utility vehicle I will show operation of the "Push button power folding third row seat that folds flat in under 3 seconds" or the operation of the cargo shade. This is also a great time to point out if the vehicle is equipped with a "Rear-Entertainment system that allows rear seat passengers to watch DVD's, Blue-ray discs or media from USB or HDMI-MHL or to listen to audio from disc, USB or radio tuner. It also comes with wireless headphones that provide optimum audio to the listeners, without distracting others in the vehicle." To end the exterior walk around you want to finish up at the driver's door and open it for the prospect to sit in the driver's seat.

Once the prospect is sitting in the driver's seat, I assist them with getting comfortable in vehicle. This step serves three purposes – 1. It's a safety issue because I don't want my prospects adjusting their mirrors, seat or steering wheel during the test drive, therefore distracting them from driving safely. 2. By making the prospect comfortable they are more likely to enjoy the vehicle and be more inclined to complete the purchase. 3. It's an opportunity to point out desirable features like the heated, power tilt and telescoping steering wheel, the heated and cooled 22-way power front seats with 9 different massage settings, or the remote power folding outside rear view mirrors that are also heated and equipped with "Side Blind Zone Alert." When I'm finished assisting the prospect with adjusting everything to their liking, I will store the settings into the seat memory for their driving preferences, as well as explain the exit memory and store that for them as well. By doing this I've shown a couple more "WOW" factors and if I close the deal it's a couple less steps I need to complete during delivery. Also, if the vehicle is equipped with Head Up Display (HUD) I will be sure to explain that feature and make sure the client sees it, knows how it works and has it adjusted properly. Another "WOW" factor. So, you might be asking yourself – "What if the vehicle I'm selling isn't equipped with all of those high-end luxury options?" Well, I will demonstrate the features the vehicle does have. Instead of demonstrating the power seats, I will show them how the seat manually adjusts. If it doesn't have a power steering wheel, I will show them the manual adjustment, etc....

Next, I will tell the prospect – "That was a brief overview for this side of the vehicle so I will hop into the passenger seat and provide you with an overview of the infotainment system, climate controls and a few other interior features." If the prospect is accompanied by a spouse, children or friends I will politely ask them – "Do you mind if I sit in the front passenger seat so I can provide all of you with a brief description of the infotainment system and climate controls?" Very rarely will they decline the offer as most people want to know how those features work, so they are able to form their own opinion. Once I'm sitting in the front passenger seat, the first thing I do is ask the prospect what temperature they prefer for their climate control and then show them how to adjust the system to their preferred setting. If equipped with the "tri-zone" climate control I will ask the rear passengers what they prefer and if there are no rear passengers, I simply show the driver how they can adjust the climate controls for the rear passengers.

Once my prospects have their preferred climate settings set, I ask them what their favorite radio station is so I can show them how to find it, store it as a favorite and have them listening to something they enjoy. More and more often as time marches on, I'm having prospects tell me they no longer listen to the radio because they stream from their mobile devices. When this happens, I use it as an opportunity to show them how to pair their phone to the vehicle infotainment system via Bluetooth so I'm able to demonstrate how easy it is to stream from their own device. Now that the client is enjoying their own favorite radio station or streaming their favorite music, I show them how to enter a navigation destination via the factory navigation system, if equipped. I'll show them both the manual entry method as well as by voice. After I use the voice commands I will say – "It even understands my Wisconsin accent, pretty impressive, eh?" This always gets a laugh since there is a definite difference in English accents between Wisconsin and Illinois people. Since I spent the first 34 years of my life in WI, I still have my Wisconsin accent and prospects and clients still ask me if I'm from WI, Minnesota or Canada. Anyway, it's another great time to deploy some humor and keep my prospects happy by keeping them laughing. If not equipped with factory navigation, I demonstrate the mobile phone interfacing apps and how they are able to project the GPS map from their phone as well as music apps, messaging and utilizing their phone's voice search via the steering wheel controls.

The whole point of showing the prospect all these features (not just showing but also demonstrating) is to get them excited about the capabilities of the vehicle and to differentiate myself from most of the other car salespeople out there. I see some salespeople just hand the keys to the customer, open the door to the car and tell them to have a great time on their test drive and not even go with them! They still sell cars but they're not building value in themselves as an expert sales consultant and they're not building value in the vehicle they're trying to sell. There's an old saying in the car business – "More time selling equals less time negotiating" and I have found it to be true. Clients do pay more if they're excited about the product and if they want the product. Nobody in this world needs a luxury vehicle however a lot of them want a luxury vehicle and the more features I show them, the more they want it. The more upgraded amenities, options, technology and safety features I show them or mention, the more excited they become about owning the vehicle and they want it even more. The more the prospect or client wants it, the more they will pay. It's quite common for prospects to enter the showroom and immediately ask "What's the best price of this vehicle?" I'll respond – "Let's find out", then offer a handshake and a HUGE smile (remember the meet and greet I wrote about earlier) and politely tell them to have a seat at my desk and begin my consultation. If the prospect says "All I want is your best price" I assure them that we will provide a great price however we need to first determine if the vehicle is the right vehicle for them. I will often say to them – "A great price is not so great if you end up buying a car you don't like" and this usually makes sense to them, so we are able to proceed with the consultation and following steps. Sometimes the client is pressed for time or just plain doesn't want to cooperate so in those cases I will just cut to the chase and get the best price from my manager and hope for the best. The odds of these types of clients returning are slim however it does occasionally happen. I try to do everything I can to stick with my process to increase my odds of selling the car and increasing my profit margin. More time selling equals less time negotiating.

Now on to the test drive. I'm guessing that 99% of the test drives I assist my clients with are the exact same route. When I began my car sales career, the dealership I work for provided a defined test drive route that takes about 10 minutes and I've stuck with it ever since. It's not too long and not too short. The route works well because it consists mostly of right turns which are safer than left turns. It incorporates a couple of miles of highway so the prospect can drive the car at highway speed and try out the adaptive cruise control or semi-autonomous cruise control features, if equipped.

To begin, I provide a brief overview of the route. I tell them where we are going and explain why we're going that way, so the route makes sense to them. I say it like this – "The best route to take for a test drive is to go North on Hwy 59, then West on Hwy 14 so you can drive the car at highway speeds." The prospect almost always says "Sounds great" or "OK" or "Sounds like a plan", or something to that effect, and off we go. On a rare occasion, the client just doesn't listen or insists on taking the vehicle to their home to show their spouse and that's ok, however if I take too little or too much time on the test drive this can negatively impact my ability to close the deal. If the test drive isn't long enough then the prospect won't get enough feel for the car and they won't have as much time to take mental ownership of the new vehicle. The longer the client drives the new car the more they think about where they will drive it and how the vehicle will incorporate into their life. If they take too much time though, then this adds time to my deal and as one of my former managers said – "Too much time is death to a deal!"

Once my prospect is test driving the vehicle, I will start asking "trial close" questions to determine if the vehicle is the right vehicle for them. Many times, it is obvious from the start that the client loves the vehicle so not many (if any) trial close questions are needed and I can just enjoy the ride. Most of the time. I won't get into discussions of scary test drives with prospects driving dangerously, however, I have been told by management more than once, that as a sales consultant, I do have the right to end a test drive at any time if the prospect is driving dangerously. No car deal is worth losing your life because the prospect thinks they know how to drive like a professional race car driver. Fortunately, I have not had to end any test drives, however I have scolded a few prospects for driving too fast and firmly told them to slow down. I say – "Our dealership policy is no speeding on test drives, please slow down!"

The first trial close question/s I ask after we've driven a couple of blocks is – "How does it feel?" or "Are you comfortable?" Most of the time they say "good" or "great", or "Yes, it's very comfy." and sometimes they will provide negative feedback such as "I'm too low" or "I'm too high" or "this car has big blind spots." If the issue is a seat position issue I will instruct the prospect to pull over at the next available safe place and assist them in adjusting the seat, steering wheel, foot pedals or whatever it is, to a more comfortable position, and promptly resume the test drive. Many times, if the concern is something like the blind spots are too big, it's an opportunity to turn it into a positive. I use the blind spot example because it is a common concern of my clients. Fortunately, almost all new models I sell have the side blind zone alert system so once I mention this feature and how it works, the prospect is now excited to have this new feature their old vehicle didn't have and more likely to buy the car. Granted, many of my clients have had this feature previously and this is not an issue however this is just one of many examples I could make about how a simple trial close question can improve your odds of making a sale vs. not saying anything and the issue is something the client never mentions and keeps inside them as a negative feeling toward the vehicle.

Another trial close question I like to ask during the test drive is – "What will be your main purpose for this vehicle?" This question prompts the prospect to think about driving the vehicle for their morning or evening commute to work, taking the kids to sporting events, pulling into Church on Sunday morning, or wherever they plan on going. This also gets them thinking how much more enjoyable it will be in the new vehicle vs their old one and again, make them more likely to buy the vehicle. This also prompts the prospect to tell you a bit more about themselves and what they do with their life so it's another opportunity to build rapport. I see it as an opportunity to get to know my prospects better or reconnect with my repeat clients and catch up with them on what's happening in their life. I've found that most people really appreciate it when I take an interest in them and what they do, just as I do. When I'm trying to sell a car though, I make a point to focus on my prospect or client and make the experience about them. After all, it's the second largest purchase most people make in their life so it should be about them. I do tell a little bit about myself though, just to let them know I'm a regular guy with a wife and a son, making a living assisting with their car purchase, not the devil-horned car salesman who is only there to gouge their eyeballs out with massive profits.

Now for the bomb of trial close questions. As my prospect is pulling the vehicle back into the lot, many times they ask – "Where should I park?" My answer is – "How about the detail bay so I can have it detailed and filled with gas for you to take home?" If they don't ask where to park, I will ask them – "Should I have it detailed and gassed for you to take home?" Sometimes, the prospect or client simply says "yes" and boom, I extend my hand to seal the deal and we go inside to my desk and write it up. Most of the time, the client or prospect says – "We need to talk numbers first." Or, "You haven't even told me what my trade is worth!" My replies to these responses are – "Let's go to my desk and I will put together a proposal for you" or in response to the trade reply – "Let's go inside so we can find out what my manager has determined and we'll generate a proposal for you."

Sometimes, the prospect simply does not like the car and will let you know why. Sometimes it might be an issue you can do nothing to overcome, however many times they are simply objections that can be overcome. One example of something that can't be overcome are a client's aversion to the color of the exterior or interior. I've offered to have vehicles completely repainted however not one prospect has ever taken me up on it so I've never even found out how much it would cost. That's probably why most people just laugh at me when I suggest it. One example of an objection that can be overcome and turned into a closing question is when the prospect says the vehicle needs an alignment or has some other mechanical issue (either real or perceived.) Regardless of what the issue is, my immediate question back to the prospect or client is – "If we correct that item/s, do we have a deal?" I ask this question because they have already told me or indicated they won't buy the car because of the issue so I see it as my job to let them know it is correctable. Sometimes it might be an expensive repair such as a electromagnetic shock absorber on a 5-year-old car however I don't convince myself that cost is going to prohibit us from making a deal. I let management make that decision. Most of the time the prospect or client will respond positively and let me know that if we agree to correct the issue, they will buy the car. When this happens, I make sure that I write the condition the client is expecting to be corrected on the client offer sheet or work sheet, "we owe" form, checklist and make sure I address the issue with management verbally. I also make sure to let the client know that I need management approval to cover the cost of the correction. I do not want to be explaining to management how I agreed to replace an expensive shock absorber after the deal has been signed, sealed and delivered. If management won't or can't absorb the cost of the repair and the prospect won't buy the vehicle without it being corrected or for some other objection I'm unable to overcome, the only other option is to review the inventory and make suggestions of other vehicles to the prospect. Hopefully we have something else in inventory they are open to and if so, I start over with another walk around.

Whether it's the first vehicle I've demonstrated, and test driven with the customer or the last, once they have committed to the vehicle it's time for the negotiation and/or write up. I've been selling cars for a while now and the negotiation step has changed quite a lot over the years however the same basic principles apply. My dealership is moving toward a "one price" dealership with no negotiation and very market driven pricing however the prospects and clients still want to negotiate and are historically accustomed to negotiating vehicle pricing. At the time I write this, the negotiation step is now more of a "price justification" step. When I began my career, my manager instructed me to write up any offer made by a prospect, no matter how ridiculous. For instance, if we were asking $30,000 for a vehicle and the prospect said "I'll buy it for $20,000," I was instructed to reply – "So if we could sell it to you for $20,000 plus tax, license and documentation fee then will you complete the paperwork and take delivery right now?" Then, I would write up the customer's offer like this – "Customer offers $20,000 plus t,t,l - x_____ " and have them sign on the line by the x. Then, I would take the offer to my manager and he would cross out the clients offer, and hand write a number somewhere in between and send me back with "great news!" I would come back to my desk where the client was sitting and say, "Great news, I got you a $500 discount!" And back and forth we would go until we reached an agreement. These days, I have to be more of an educator to the clients and explain how the internet has changed our industry, making it more competitive and market driven so if there is any room to discount, it would be in hundreds of dollars, not thousands. Therefore, not as much room to negotiate, if any.

The dealership I work for has made this very easy to accomplish by providing real time market data I can share with my clients to justify our pricing. I show them all the vehicles within a specific search radius generated by software that shows the client how our vehicle is priced competitively. Most of the time, they already know this and that is why they visited, because our price is competitive. With that said, a lot of customers still want to negotiate so if I've done my best to justify our price and the client is still insisting on a discount or making a ridiculous offer, I revert to my old school tactics of writing up their offer and letting management have an opportunity to justify our pricing, based on the market data. I always try to solicit an offer from the prospect that is higher than their original offer, explaining how the market has changed and I can't promise them that we are able to improve on our price since it's already competitive, however I will do my best for them and try to convince my manager to accept their offer, but it needs to be a reasonable offer. I'll go for the "split" – "If we could split the difference, do we have a deal?" Whether they agree to the split or won't budge, I write it up, have the prospect sign it, and take it to "the boss". At this point, my boss (manager) will get involved and re-justify our pricing for the client. Most managers were great salespeople and that is why they're managers. Because they know how to close deals and make the deal make sense for the customer, so the customer agrees to buy the vehicle. Therefore, I always try to get my managers involved in my deals. Often, they will mention something to the prospect that I didn't think of or offer an alternative payment scenario and bingo, it makes sense to the prospect and we have a deal!

In most instances now, our vehicle is already the least expensive of all similar vehicles so management will "stick to their guns" and not discount and many times, the customer realizes at that point that they are not getting a discount however since we have justified our price based on real market data, they agree to buy the vehicle for our price, with no discount. These days, the consumer has so many online resources available to them to conduct their research that they know what a fair deal is and wouldn't have spent their time and energy visiting our dealership if our prices weren't competitive. In this regard, selling cars has become easier in terms of new business coming into the store, already having pre-qualified themselves on a specific vehicle.

Another intangible trait I feel has made me a good car sales consultant is my ability to make my clients feel at ease during the negotiation. Many prospects are very nervous about negotiating or discussing pricing because it's a very big purchase for them and they are going to be spending a large amount of their hard-earned money. They want to be sure they are making the right decision and not "getting screwed." I've had several managers compliment me on how non-threatening I am while I'm negotiating because I'm very laid back. I never really thought about it until the second manager mentioned it to me. I tend to tilt back in my chair while justifying our pricing, so I it makes my prospects and clients more at ease and therefore, more comfortable, and more likely to say "yes!" Some salespeople are more in your face and like to try to impose their will and intimidate their customers into buying and although I've seen those types of tactics work, I don't think it makes the client feel good about the transaction. So, in my humble opinion they won't become repeat clients and they're not going to provide you with a nice 5- star review online. I haven't mentioned repeat clients in a while however they are THE reason for my long-term success selling cars.

Once the client says yes to the price, that is the point in the road to the sale that I consider the deal "closed." There's an old acronym called "ABC" and it stands for "Always Be Closing" and I still don't quite understand this because in my opinion, asking for the sale must be done at the right time. The right time could be very early in your contact with the client, very late, or anywhere in between so maybe that is why the saying is "ABC." For instance, an example of an early close is when I have an internet client who has only provided their email address for contact information however in their initial inquiry they offer to purchase our vehicle if we agree to shipping the vehicle to their location two States away from our dealership. The shipping could cost $500 - $1,000 so it's something we typically can't do however I will respond by letting them know I don't think that's possible since our vehicle is already priced aggressively relative to the market, however – "If I could convince my manager to pay the shipping will you wire the funds to pay for the vehicle right away?" If the client responds with a "yes" then I let them know I will present their offer and let them know what my manager says. My manager might say no however he might say – "I'll take $200 off for them. If he says this, I call my customer back and let them know that I have "great news, my manager took $200 off!" I consider any discount as great news for my clients since I truly believe that I am worth more than sticker price. Why am I worth more? Because I care about my clients and I show it from the moment I greet them to the time I say goodbye, watch them drive off in their newly purchased vehicle, and after the sale. By greeting them with a big smile, getting to know them, and sincerely doing my best to make their experience the best car buying experience they've ever had, before and after they take delivery, I believe sticker price is fair to both parties. With that said, if the client doesn't buy the car for sticker price then I must do everything I can to make the deal. "A little bit of something is better than a whole lot of nothing." If my manager can't discount, then that's the way it is, and I will politely explain this to the prospect and let them know I wish I could do better however it doesn't make good business sense for the dealership.

If I'm unable to convince the client to make an offer or accept management's counteroffer, then it's time for the "T.O." T.O. stands for "turn-over." A T.O. is when I get my manager involved directly with the client to assist me with the close. A T.O. could happen at any time during the sale if there is a question I can't answer that I think my manager might be able to answer, however the most important time for a T.O. is when I need assistance to close the deal. Early on in my career I would get frustrated because I would explain something to the client that I thought would close the deal and it didn't. However, when I got my managers involved on a T.O. they would explain the exact same thing and the client would all the sudden agree to the deal based on what I already told them! After a while, I finally realized that sometimes clients need to hear the same advice from a different source to reinforce the message so makes sense to them. Another common occurrence with a T.O. is that the manager will offer a different idea for the client that makes more sense to them, enough for them to agree to buy the car. For instance, they might recommend a longer payment term, a lesser equipped model or they might know of an inbound trade that makes more sense for the client. Or, once again, the client might just need to hear the same exact thing from a different source to convince them it's the right thing to do. One big thing the manager could do is adjust the pricing to make the deal for me. This reduces my commission however if the client isn't willing to agree to buy the vehicle for the price before the manager discounts it what good is that to me to have no deal? If the manager's discount closes the deal, I'm all for it because it's a minimum $200 commission and that is better than no commission!

Once I've sold the vehicle, I also now have an opportunity to sell the client an environmental protection package as well as earn manufacturer spiffs for things like successful telematics enrollment or performance-based spiffs from the manufacturer. Every year my accountant says to me during our tax meeting – "Wow, you had another good year of spiffs!" He knows how much I earn in spiffs because I receive a 1099 form from the manufacturer since the spiffs are paid directly to me and not taxed by the dealership like my regular pay. Spiffs make up about 12% - 15% of my gross income so it's a substantial amount of money. Spiffs do not come easy however I make sure I pay attention to the programs and what's required of me to earn them. As an example, if I sell any used vehicle and enroll the client in the telematics system and make sure they press the telematics button in the vehicle then I earn $20 per used vehicle. If I sell 3 new vehicles in a one month time frame I earn an extra $100 per vehicle, provided I've enrolled them in the telematics, make sure they sign up for the manufacturer's rewards program, my online training is completed and current, and my customer satisfaction scores are above the manufacturer's minimum requirement. If I sell a fourth new vehicle, I earn an additional $100 per vehicle so up to $200 extra per new vehicle if I meet all the criteria. Therefore, the $200 minimum commission (mini) becomes a $400 mini. It's not easy and it takes effort however I'm living proof that even an uneducated slouch can do it! I've only worked for one dealership and one manufacturer however I'm sure most, if not all manufacturers offer similar bonus or "spiff" programs. My dealership even pays me $20 if I get a 5-star review from my clients. All I must do is remember to send the review link to my clients and politely ask them to complete a quick 5-star review for me. Getting back to the point – if I don't close the deal or the manager doesn't close the deal for me, I don't get a commission or the opportunity to earn spiffs.

Once the deal is closed, whether I closed it on my own or with the manager's assistance, I now must assemble the required paperwork the finance manager will need to "bill out" the deal. "Bill out" simply means having the client sign all the required legal documents to take ownership of the vehicle. My dealership has always had some sort of checklist that shows me all the required documents so it's fairly simple – driver's license, current insurance card, credit application, vehicle registration card for the trade, exact miles on both new vehicle and trade, and the we owe form. The finance manager will let me know if I missed any forms, however I always do my best to ensure I have all the necessary paperwork assembled properly. By doing this, the finance manager doesn't have to waste time chasing me for documents and therefore, doesn't waste the client's time, making for a happier client. Yes, I'm going to say it again – happy clients equal repeat clients!

Another important thing to focus on is keeping your client occupied while the finance manager is preparing the formal paperwork. It takes time for the finance manager to prepare so I always make sure I let the client know it will take some time. Secondly, I make sure I stay engaged with the client during this time. There are several things I do while we're waiting for the finance manager. One thing is to enroll the client in the telematics program if the vehicle is equipped. Since I work for a new vehicle franchise, most of the vehicles I sell are new, CPO or used models of the same brand and a lot of other used brands from the same manufacturer. All those brands have the same telematics system and once the client is enrolled through the online enrollment process and presses the telematics button in their new vehicle, I earn another $20. Not bad for doing something that benefits the customer and keeps them occupied while waiting for the finance manager. The brand-new models I sell also require completion of a sales assistant app that is basically another checklist of everything that needs to be explained and demonstrated to the client. The assistant app is a requirement not only for my manufacturer spiff, it is also a requirement for the dealership's manufacturer bonus money so it must be done and the time between the close and the business office is the perfect time to complete it since it is not only required, it also keeps my clients occupied and not watching the clock. If the vehicle I've sold is used and a brand other than from our new vehicle manufacturer there are other things I do to keep my clients engaged. One is to have the client clean out and organize their trade vehicle. If I wait until the new vehicle detail is completed and the paperwork is done, I've seen it take clients up to half an hour just to get their old car cleaned out so if we wait until the paperwork is done this step now adds more time to the clients process and the longer the process takes, the less satisfied the client will be. Some clients have their trade vehicle already cleaned out and it doesn't take them more than a minute to gather the few belongings they have in the vehicle so if this is the case, it's time to fall back on offering drinks, snacks and making small talk until the finance manager is ready to assist them with the paperwork.

Most car salespeople have their clients sit in the waiting area and ignore them while waiting to do their paperwork however I prefer to sit with them to keep them occupied. My opinion is, if I place them in the waiting area, they feel like they're at the dentist or doctor's office, being ignored and watching the clock continue ticking. I don't like waiting in a waiting area and I don't think many people do so by staying with my clients I think it provides a more hospitable feeling. I also see it as an opportunity to further build and cement our relationship. Once the finance manager has the formal paperwork prepared, they will come greet the client and escort them to the business office to complete the paperwork. Once the client has completed the paperwork in the business office it is now time for the "delivery."

Chapter 5: Dazzle 'Em at Delivery

Now that the deal is closed and the client has completed their paperwork in the finance office, it's time to "dazzle 'em at delivery!" How I conduct my delivery process is probably the single biggest reason for my high number of repeat clients. I've had too many clients to count tell me after I've completed the delivery of the vehicle to them, that it was the best experience they've ever had buying a car. I've even had several clients cry tears of joy because they were so happy. I must give credit to my old friend Joe for teaching me the proper way to deliver a new vehicle. Unfortunately, Joe passed away a couple of years ago, however I will never forget him and how helpful he was in taking me under his wing when I started selling cars. I took what Joe taught me though and tweaked it to make it my own and give it my own style. It didn't happen overnight and took a while to really nail it down and make it a professional demonstration however once I had it figured out, it has become a crucial part of my complete sales process.

I had bought two brand new vehicles before I started selling cars and in both cases I was very excited to be buying a brand-new car. I was very proud of myself for what I had done to earn the ability to buy a new car, so it was a big deal. In both instances, the salesman that sold me the car really didn't share in the excitement and basically just flipped me the keys. I'm not even sure if they thanked me. I certainly don't remember them doing anything to make it special so once I was shown by Joe how a new vehicle should be properly delivered, I thought to myself that I would do my best to make it the best experience my clients ever had taking delivery of a new car.

The first thing I do to make the delivery special is to make sure the new vehicle is perfect. While my clients are in the business office signing the formal paperwork, I conduct a final inspection of the vehicle to ensure it is perfectly clean, inside and out. If I find something the detail staff missed, such as dirt on the door sill, dust on the dash, or fingerprints, I politely point it out to them, and they are glad to correct it. Many times, I will just grab a cloth and clean it myself to save time and show the detailers that I'm not afraid to jump in and help them. I always have tried to treat people well and have realized that not all salespeople treat the detail staff like they should. They boss them around and simply aren't very nice. Since I treat them nicely and help them when they need it, I rarely have a problem with them doing insufficient work for me. The detail staff can "make or break" my delivery by having the car ready on time and cleaned perfectly or not. If the client is forced to sit around and wait another 30 minutes once they have completed their paperwork because their new car isn't ready, it doesn't make them feel like it was a great experience so they will be less likely to provide me with a positive online review or perfect CSI survey, or become a repeat client. Beyond the client being happy, it's just common courtesy in my mind that since my clients are spending thousands of dollars (sometimes over $100,000) on their new vehicle, it should be perfect the first time they see it after they've just "signed their life away" for it. Even if it's a $5,000 car I make sure it is as nice as it could possibly be because it is still new to my client.

Once my client's new car is perfect, ready for delivery, and they have completed their paperwork, it's time for me to dazzle 'em on the features and capability of their new vehicle. Sometimes, the client is in a rush to leave since they've already been at the dealership for about 2-3 hours, on average. If this is the case, I let them know it's no problem and encourage them to come back when they can make time so I can assist them with acquiring a full understanding of the capabilities of their new ride. Even if they do go through the full tutorial, I let them know they're welcome back any time to go through the vehicle again if they have any questions, concerns or want to change any of the personalization settings.

The first thing I do is point out important features on the exterior of the vehicle. The main features are the fuel filler door, the trunk release, the spare tire (if equipped) or tire inflator kit, hood release, battery terminals for jump starting (I say terminals because many vehicles have the battery in the trunk so there are only jumper terminals under the hood), and where to fill the windshield wiper fluid. I'll also point out where the camera lenses are located and inform the client that the lenses could be compromised by dirt, ice, or snow. Very importantly, I point out the camera located in the upper part of the windshield because this camera is part of the lane departure warning and collision systems so if it is covered in dirt, ice or snow it could completely disable those safety features, rendering them useless. At this time, I always advise my clients that I suggest they only use the safety features as a back up to good driving habits like maintaining a safe following distance with the vehicle in front of them and turning their head to check their blind spot before making a lane change, as well as using their turn signals.

The next thing I do is demonstrate how to operate the rear lift gate or trunk. You might think – really, you have to show them how to open the lift gate?" Yes, because most of the vehicles I sell have a power lift gate and different models have different touch pad locations to open them or might even be equipped with "hands free lift gate" that allows them to open it by waiving their foot beneath the rear bumper. The touch pads are in different areas of the lift gate or trunk and the hands-free operation also has different areas the client needs to waive their foot, depending on which model they are buying. For instance, there is a sedan model I sell that utilizes the logo located on the trunk as the trunk release so the client very easily could have a difficult time finding it. Could you imagine a client going to the grocery store for the first time with their new vehicle and can't put their groceries in it because they don't know how to open the trunk? Talk about frustration that could lead to a bad CSI survey. I don't want that happening! For the SUV's and crossover vehicles I sell, there is also a button on the remote that needs to be pressed twice to open the lift gate and the old models only required one press so that could be a sticking point too. It shows on the remote (x 2) indicating the button requires a double press however the print is very small and could easily not be seen. Once the rear lift gate is open, I will demonstrate the operation of the third-row seat if equipped as well as pointing out any cargo organizers, cargo covers, cargo net, and the spare tire or tire inflator kit.

Next, I show them the interior of the vehicle. I begin by opening the drivers' door for the client and have them sit in the drivers' seat. In most cases, I've already had the client adjust their seat, mirrors, steering wheel (and foot pedals if adjustable) at the beginning of the test drive so all

I need to do is confirm with the client that these items are adjusted to their preference and show them again how to store their memory settings. Even if I had done this at the beginning of the test drive, I show them again, just to reinforce what I showed them so they will be able to do it themselves, after they leave the dealership. I also ensure we have identified the keys as "driver one" and "driver two" to ensure the client has the correct key for their settings. For the brand I sell, the majority of the vehicles have keys that are individually coded to recall the memory settings so if the client has stored their settings as driver one and they start the vehicle with the driver two key the vehicle will recall the wrong settings. If this happens the client could become frustrated and reflect that on the CSI survey as a negative experience. A negative CSI score could cost me money because if my CSI isn't on par with the manufacturers criteria, I could lose 50% of my bonus. The manufacturer bonus money the dealership earns is also dependent on CSI so it could cost the dealership a very significant amount of money and obviously, I don't want to be the one who costs the dealership it's bonus money. Fortunately, my CSI scores are very high because I make a conscious effort to ensure the customer is "completely satisfied." I make it a point throughout the entire process to mention to the client that my goal is to ensure they have a positive experience and are "completely satisfied." I'll typically mention it at least two or three times throughout the sales process. For instance, as I'm figuring out which key is for driver one and which key is for driver two, I will say something like this to the client – "Now we're going to determine which key is for driver one and which key is for driver two so I make sure that when you start your vehicle it recalls the correct memory settings for you. This is very important because I need to ensure you are completely satisfied and will be able to reflect that on your customer satisfaction survey you will be receiving soon. More importantly, I need to ensure you are completely satisfied so you become another one of my highly valued repeat clients."

The next part of the delivery is providing the client with a very thorough understanding of their infotainment system. The "infotainment system" on the new models I sell are essentially the same across all models so for the last 6 years I've essentially only had to know one system. Prior to that, there were three different infotainment systems I had to learn thoroughly. I had to learn them because if I don't know them myself, how could I show my clients how to operate them? Anyway, it's much easier to just learn one system. When the system was first introduced, I sat in the first vehicle we took inventory of with the new system and sat in the car and learned every icon, button and operation it offered. This system is very similar to a smart phone or tablet so it's actually very easy to operate however there are simple tips and tricks I learned by reading the manual and by showing and demonstrating these tips and tricks it could make a big difference when it comes to CSI. The other major impact my knowledge of the infotainment system provides is the WOW factor it provides for the client, building value in the vehicle and building value in me as a smart, knowledgeable, and professional car sales consultant. Therefore, I'm building brand loyalty to the vehicles I sell and more importantly, brand loyalty to me. That's right. I'm my own brand and that's how I see it so I'm constantly focusing on doing the little things to make my clients car buying experience great, so my clients are more likely to become the coveted repeat clients!

Back to the infotainment system. Like most vehicle systems today, the system in the vehicles I sell contains the radio, CD operation (if equipped because CD is becoming obsolete), media, navigation, climate controls, personalization settings, Bluetooth, and many other apps from newspapers to weather. In most instances, I have already demonstrated the infotainment features during the demonstration drive however during the vehicle delivery I will go through them again, starting with the climate controls. Where I work in northern Illinois it can be -25F up to over 100F so most of the time I'm either trying to warm up the vehicle or cool down the vehicle for my client. In either case, I begin by asking my client what their preferred cabin temperature is and follow by showing them how to adjust the controls to achieve their preference. I'm a big believer that a client comfortable with the climate will be more comfortable the vehicle and with me.

The next feature I focus on is the radio. Once again, during the demonstration drive, I usually show the client how to select a station and store it into their favorites so most of the time I am reiterating how to do it. Then I show them how to navigate between favorites. I also ensure they know how to switch between bands and adjust their sound settings such as bass, midrange, treble, other equalizer settings and balance/fade. I point out the media icon as well, so they know how to stream music from their smart phone. With the infotainment system I sell, on the satellite band, there is even a way to display not only the station, but the artist playing currently as well as the song title, so I make sure I show my clients how to display each, another W.O.W factor.

Following the radio, I demonstrate to the client how to pair their phone to the vehicle via Bluetooth. I always insist on pairing the phone for the client so I can ensure it is done properly, especially allowing the vehicle to access the client's phone book so they will have the ability to voice dial their contacts via the voice command button located on the steering wheel. If the client isn't properly taught how to operate the Bluetooth system, it could be a source of dissatisfaction and they could negatively reflect that on their CSI survey. If this is done properly and the client has a firm understanding of this operation it becomes a reinforcer of their love of their vehicle and their sales consultant, here again more likely to become a repeat client.

The next feature I demonstrate is the factory navigation system. First off, I show how to access the navigation page. Secondly, I show how to change the map view since most clients prefer either North up, heading up, or birds eye view. I'll show my clients all three views and ask them which one they prefer and I'm often surprised to learn that they weren't aware it was even possible to change the view and they've been living with a non-preferred view for the entire time they've owned their previous vehicle. Big win for me when this happens because I'm further cementing my value as a professional and once again, building more value in the brand of vehicle I sell. I then show them how to enter a destination by voice as well as manually type it in and mention that they could also have the live telematics advisor enter a destination for them as they are driving. I always ask if we could use their home address so once it's entered, I could show them how to store it as a favorite. Once entered, I show them how to store it as a favorite so they will be able to easily select it with one touch from that moment forward. WOW! I also show the navigation preference menu that allows the client to adjust their traffic preferences and voice prompts. One other important feature that is simple to figure out that I show anyway, is the zoom feature – how to adjust the scale of the map. And that's about it for navigation however the simple step of taking a couple of minutes to show these features to my clients is something I'm pretty confident most of my competition isn't doing and it's most likely something the client's last salesperson didn't do, unless it was me, which is the case, more and more often as my career advances. Oh yeah. Repeat client's baby!

Following the navigation demo, I get my clients involved in the settings menu. The settings menu is a great opportunity to WOW my clients because once again, this is something I'm confident most car sales consultants do not do and it's huge in making the difference between someone buying a new car and someone having the best new car purchase experience they've ever had. I go through each setting and there are too many to list however the main sections are comfort and convenience, vehicle, safety and security, lighting, and locking/unlocking. Each one of these main sections has sub settings and I know it leaves a lasting impression on my clients once I explain everything to them and personalize all the settings to their preferences. For instance, I make sure in the comfort and convenience section that the memory recall is turned on for both driving and entry/exit of the vehicle and I make sure it is set to recall when the client wants it to. With many clients, they prefer the seat and steering wheel don't move when they enter, start or exit the vehicle so for those clients I make sure those features are turned off. It's all about personalizing the vehicle to act how the client wants it to act, therefore making for very happy and completely satisfied customers.

Another very cool feature included on the vehicles I sell are the phone interface apps. I make sure I show my clients all the other pre-installed apps in their infotainment system and then demonstrate the internet interfacing apps. The phone interfacing apps enable a car radio or head unit to be a display and act as a controller for the client's smart phone. These apps have been standard on all the new models I sell since the middle of 2015 so I'm now starting to gain some decent feedback on what my clients think and more and more of them are using these apps rather than the factory display so it's crucial that I show all of my clients how to use them. The great news is that it's very easy to explain, demonstrate and initiate for the client. All I need to do is connect their smart phone to one of the USB ports in the vehicle, accept one prompt on the vehicle infotainment touch screen and one prompt on the client's phone. Once that is done, the client's infotainment screen looks very similar to the client's phone. The client can now begin to utilize the app.

One very big advantage in my opinion is that since the interfacing apps allow the user to project their GPS map from their phone to their vehicle's infotainment screen there really is no need for the vehicle to be equipped with the factory navigation system although I do encounter many clients who still prefer the factory navigation option vs their phone maps so it really boils down to personal preference of the client. The first thing I do once the clients phone interface app is activated is ask the client to excuse my reach while I press and hold the voice button the steering wheel and wait for the voice command chime.

Then I will give a command asking directions to a popular hot dog joint or pizza place. It usually takes 2-3 hours to complete a car purchase so it is very common for my clients to ask me where they could go to grab a bite to eat once the deal is wrapping up. Here in the Chicago suburbs where I work, two of the popular items people like to indulge in are Chicago style hot dogs and Chicago style deep dish pizza so I figure I can't go wrong in entering one of those into the client's navigation system. I think it makes people happy to think of hot dogs and pizza because in this day of health consciousness it gives people sort of celebratory feeling. What better way to celebrate a new vehicle purchase than by indulging in junk food!

This book is taking me so long to write that it's possible this technology will be obsolete by the time I get it published however my point in showing each and every feature and the technology in the client's new vehicle is to impress the client with the capabilities of their new vehicle like no other salesperson has done for them previously or subsequently. I try to make their experience the best they've ever had so they return for future vehicles and my method has worked, generating a consistent flow of repeat clients and referrals that returns multiple deals, month after month, after month. The phone interfacing apps have only been around for a few years however I've adapted to the changing technology and will continue to do so because it is critical to being able to differentiate myself from my competition. Before these apps were around, I was always up to speed on knowing the technology of the vehicle and made sure I demonstrated it to my clients. Back in 2004 which doesn't sound like that long ago for an old guy like me, a 6-disc CD changer was a big deal so I would show my clients how to load and eject their CD's into or out of the system. I even had to show them where the CD changer was located. Some were in the trunk, some were in the glove box and if the vehicle had an in-dash changer that was a real WOW factor! The navigation system of the day had a toggle switch to navigate the cursor on the map so that was a real WOW factor. Another technology that was introduced during my tenure selling cars was Bluetooth. Now standard on most vehicles, it was a big deal if a car was equipped with Bluetooth back in 2005. It was a huge WOW factor when I would pair my client's phone and demonstrate to them how they could make and receive phone calls with simple voice commands. The pairing process was cumbersome back then and the voice commands had to be very specific, so it took some effort and practice to master the system and be able to demonstrate it successfully. The very cool thing is that many of those clients I demonstrated Bluetooth to back in the mid 2000's continues to buy cars from me now. In fact, yesterday a client bought a new 2019 model and traded in a 2008 model that I sold to them originally and he provided me with the manual to his accessory Bluetooth system that we installed for them because that vehicle didn't offer it as a factory option. I remember clearly having those accessory Bluetooth systems installed for my clients and showing them how to use them and I guarantee that because I took the time to show this client how to use the system and made him comfortable with it is one of the many reasons why he bought another vehicle from me 11 years later. By the way, he bought his wife a car from me in between too, so this was the third vehicle I've sold them in 11 years. One of my many repeat clients I earned by taking the extra time to WOW them with all the little things.

One more feature of the delivery that I've always focused on and made sure to assist my clients with is the built-in remote clients can use to program their garage door and privacy gate remotes into the vehicle. This feature allows the client to program their garage door or privacy gate remote control into buttons located in the vehicle ceiling, so they no longer must have the factory remote hanging on their sun visor or sitting in their cupholder. It's a feature that most clients really like although many of them have difficulty programming it, so they don't even use it and still have the remote hanging on the visor or sitting in the cup holder of the vehicle they've been driving for several years. I used to be surprised at how many of my prospects would have this feature in the vehicle they were trading and still have their remote hanging on the visor. I am no longer surprised though because I know it's because the salesperson who sold them the last car didn't mention it and obviously didn't program it for them. If they had done that as well as completed the rest of the vehicle delivery as I do, there's a great chance these clients would be back, buying another vehicle from them, not me. Going a step further and beyond my client's expectations, I will always offer to come to my client's home (provided they're not a prohibitive distance from the dealership) and program the system for them if they have difficulty doing it themselves. Many have taken me up on this offer and are super appreciative once I get it handled for them and it shows them that I will go the "extra mile" for them.

My point is that whatever the technology de jour is, I see it as vital to my success to know it and be able to demonstrate it comfortably to my clients. I say demonstrate it comfortably because if I'm not comfortable and fumbling through my presentations I will appear unprepared and unprofessional. I'm sure I would still sell cars and I see other salespeople all the time who are exactly that and still sell cars, however those other salespeople do not reap the rewards of repeat and referral clients, as I have.

In my humble opinion, the most important facet of a successful new vehicle delivery circles back to knowing my product. Not just knowing it, but knowing how to demonstrate it, how to show it to my clients and ensure they are comfortable with it. If I don't know my product, it's capabilities and how it works, then how could I demonstrate it and show my clients how to use it? The more time I invest in my product knowledge, practice using it and ultimately sharing it with my clients, the more professional my delivery will be. I wrote this earlier in the book and it's worth writing again – when a new model first arrives at my dealership the first thing I do is sit in the car and make sure I learn and know how to use every feature and setting in the vehicle, and how to demonstrate it. Once I know it, it's easy to provide my clients with all the answers they need, a smooth and professional walk around and test drive, and a first-class new vehicle delivery that builds value in my product and more importantly, me.

Once I've completed the in-cabin portion of the delivery it's time to wrap it up. The first thing I do is sincerely thank the client for buying a car from me. Secondly, I will ask them if they have any questions I didn't answer. If they have any unanswered questions, I provide the answers or let them know I will get them the answers. The third thing I do is let them know to expect a Customer Satisfaction Index survey (CSI) via email and if there is any reason at all they are not able to provide me with an absolutely perfect, completely satisfied score then please let me know why before they submit the survey. I must ensure their 100% complete satisfaction so they can provide an absolutely perfect survey for me and the dealership. This has worked very well for me. In fact, I checked my CSI score for the last 12 months and I'm at 95%. If that 10% of clients are never satisfied rule is true, then I'd say my approach is working well. Once I confirm my client is completely satisfied, I thank them again and let them know it is time for their telematics welcome call. I let them know I'm going to press their telematics button and a live advisor will be coming on the line through the vehicle speakers to assist them with activating their free telematics trial as well as explaining what is included in the free trial. I let my client know that once I press the button, I will be exiting the vehicle and I let them know I will be following up the next day to make sure everything is going smoothly with their new vehicle. As I exit the vehicle, I tell them "thank you" once again, "enjoy your new vehicle" and "drive safely." This is also a perfect time to ask for referrals, so I always try to remember to let my clients know that I'm here to assist any of their friends and family when they need a vehicle. If I've done my job well and dazzled my client, they will send their friends and family to purchase vehicles from me. Because I care, because I genuinely try to make it the best car buying experience they've ever had, and because I ask, many of my clients send their friends and family to me for their vehicles too. So that pretty much covers my new vehicle delivery process.

Most everything I mentioned previously regarding delivery was for new vehicles. If I'm delivering a CPO vehicle or a non-CPO that is the same brand as the new and CPO I sell, I will do the same delivery, primarily because I know the brand in depth. By conducting the same delivery process for those vehicles, I build value in the brand I'm selling and I build more value in myself. This has proven to bring clients back to see me again and again because most automotive salespeople don't take the time to provide this level of service, so they don't reap the benefits of repeat and referral business nearly as much as they could. If I'm delivering a used vehicle that is an "off brand", or in other words, a vehicle that is not from the same manufacturer as the new and CPO vehicles I sell then I will not show them much because I simply don't know those vehicles very well. There are so many different makes, models and trim levels that it's impossible for me to know them all so in my opinion it's better to just hand the client the keys and thank them for their business, rather than trying to look like an expert on a vehicle when I'm not. In the next chapter I will write about the importance of follow up.

Chapter 6: Follow Up is Key!

Now I will explain how important follow up is as well as how critical it has been in the development of my loyal client base of repeat and referral clients. Once I've sold and delivered the vehicle, I always make sure that I place a follow up phone call the following day for several reasons. #1 is to confirm that my clients are happy. If there is any reason they are not happy I'm able to address their concerns and take corrective action to ensure they are happy. This builds tremendous value in me as their sales consultant because by addressing and correcting any issues promptly, it shows the client that I'm here for them and will continue to be here for them after the sale. One thing I always mention in my follow up call is to let my clients know that they are welcomed back any time for a "re-delivery" if they have any further questions on operation of any features or settings. Due to the technical complexity of vehicles these days, many of my clients take me up on this offer and are very happy once I assist them with any questions or issues they have. Here again, I'm building value to them as their sales consultant and providing a level of customer service they most likely haven't received from their previous automotive salesperson.

Another point I always make during my first follow up call is to reiterate how important the CSI survey is and how it is my "report card" so I need to earn an A++! I let them know anything less than perfect and "completely satisfied" is like an F grade. As I mentioned previously, manufacturer spiffs as well as the pay plan from my dealership are based on high scoring CSI scores so it could cost me a very significant amount of money if the customer submits a negative survey. Right now, my monthly dealership bonus could also be reduced by 50% if my scores are not on par with the level determined by the manufacturer so this is obviously very important when my bonus could be $1,000 (10 cars), $1,500 (13 cars), $2,500 (15 cars) or $5,000 (20 cars) per month. I will typically say something to this effect: "Thank you once again for allowing me to assist you with your new vehicle purchase. Please keep an eye out for a customer satisfaction survey that will be sent to you and if there is any reason or reasons you are unable to submit an absolutely perfect score for me and the dealership, please let me know why before you submit the survey. Even one question checked very satisfied rather than completely satisfied is like an F grade and more importantly, I want you to be 100% completely satisfied so you come back to see me when you're ready for your next vehicle."

The follow up phone call is also a great time to ask for referrals. I always try to remember to ask my clients for referrals at the end of my delivery process and during my follow up. If I've done my job well and the way it should be done my clients will send me referrals. Especially in the car business, people really appreciate a salesperson that genuinely cares about them, is professional, provides them with a first-class experience and follows up with them to ensure their complete satisfaction. I'm living proof and every month, a significant percentage of my sales are repeat or referral clients. I'm not a big statistics guy from the standpoint of recording or tracking things like this however I have looked back many times at my completed months sales to count how many of my sales were repeat or referral clients and many months, at least half of my deals were repeat or referral clients. It feels good to know people come back to see me for multiple purchases and send their friends and family to see me for their vehicles too. One big problem people have with car salespeople is their lack of trust in them so when one of their friends or family tells them how great I treated them they also want to do business with me. I always try to remember to "plant the seed" anyway by asking for the referral at least a couple of times, toward the end of the delivery process, as well as during my initial and subsequent follow up calls, texts, and emails.

For the first couple of years as a car salesman, I would follow up with my "old sold" clients every three months however as time has progressed and my client base has grown it has become more difficult to follow up as often because I now have so many clients if I tried to follow up with all of them that often that's all I would have time for. The great news is that now my repeat clients are following up with me. Every day I'm contacted by at least one or two, whether for service or to buy or lease another vehicle. I also see many of them in our service department and always make a point to say hello, ask them how they are doing, how their family is doing and how their car is doing. In fact, just yesterday I had two of my repeat clients stop by my desk to say hello to me while their car was being serviced. They weren't ready for a new car yet however I made time to visit with them and when they are ready, they will be back to see me. Both clients have purchased two vehicles from me previously and probably within the next year will become "threepeat" clients. As I said goodbye to them, I also made sure to let them know that I'm here to assist them with any service issues they might have in the meantime, before they're ready for their next vehicle. I think I forgot to mention it while writing about the delivery process however another thing I mention to my clients as they're taking delivery of their new vehicle is that I will be here for them after the sale if they need any assistance with scheduling service or if they have any service issues. This is a great way to stay in touch with my clients after the sale as well and many of my clients take me up on the offer. In fact, I probably schedule more service visits than our service advisors do. In addition, I'm building value in me because I don't think most salespeople provide that level of service. All they care about is the next deal they can close right now and don't see the long-term value assisting clients with their service needs provides.

Another great follow up measure is scheduling phone calls to wish clients a Happy Birthday. The last two CRM systems I've worked with at my dealership automatically prompt me when it's the clients Birthday. This is another thing I used to do consistently when I was new in the business however like the three-month follow up call, I've gotten away from it because I'm too busy working new deals and selling cars to do it now. That's a poor excuse because it doesn't take long to zip out a quick text or email to wish someone a simple "Happy Birthday" message so I'm going to try to refocus doing this. What usually happens is I see my list of "My sold customers with Birthdays within the next 7 days" and I skip past it to my follow up calendar and start working on that. Everyone loves a Birthday wish and it's powerful when someone receives a Happy Birthday message from their car salesperson. Especially when maybe one of their family members might have even forgotten to wish them a Happy Birthday. They might think – Geez, my car salesperson wished me a Happy Birthday, but my own sibling couldn't even remember!

Follow up is not only important with sold clients, it is critically important with prospective clients that I haven't sold yet. There is a term in the car business called the "be-back" and this refers to people who have visited the dealership and didn't purchase a car however they return to the dealership again another day, or maybe even make three or four return visits. Typically, if they return for a second visit, I close the deal with them however on very rare occasions, it takes three or four visits to close the deal if the prospect is overly cautious about purchasing their next vehicle. Some managers don't believe in the be-back. They say if you don't sell them on the first visit you will probably never see them again. This holds true a lot of the time however my belief is that if I treat the customer properly by doing everything I've mentioned in this book, they will appreciate me and want to buy from me, and they will "be back." If I can't close the deal, or my manager can't close the deal on the first visit, I always let them know as they're leaving that I will work on their behalf to get them the best deal they will find and provide them with the best experience both before, during, and after the sale. The biggest key though is to follow up with them to show them you want to earn their business. I know for a fact that many automotive salespeople do not follow up with prospects if they don't sell them a car on the first visit. How do I know this? Because my managers are always scolding other salespeople I work with for not following up! Not only that, I've had many customers through the years tell me they came back to buy a car from me in part due to my diligent follow up. Some clients don't want to be bothered with follow up calls and might become upset however I don't let that prevent me because most clients do appreciate it. One thing I do that I feel helps me in not upsetting my prospects is address the potential issue in my voice messages, texts and emails by saying in my messages – "I don't intend to bother you or upset you with excessive follow up however I am anxious to earn your business so please reply or call me to let me know what I could do to earn your business," or something to that effect. If the prospect is upset and doesn't want to be bothered and lets me know this, I will respect their wishes and move on to the next prospect. It's no problem because there are millions of other prospects out there in the good old USA that need a car.

Another key factor in my follow up is that I do my best to give the prospect a reason to come back and buy a car from me. I don't just leave or send a message for the sake of leaving a message. I let them know if a new incentive is being offered by the manufacturer such as a new rebate or promotional interest rate for financing, or a new lease special. If it's a used car, we might have lowered the price because the vehicle has been in inventory too long so the price might make sense for them now. Sometimes a $200 price reduction is all it takes to close the deal however if I'm not reviewing my prospect list daily, in detail, then I could miss a sale and I'm sure many of my competitors do miss sales because of this. I'm sure I have too however I try hard to not be lazy so when reviewing my prospect list, I look at all the details – have we lowered the price on a used car since the prospect was in the dealership? Has the manufacturer announced a new incentive, interest rate offer or lease deal? Sometimes the client's "hot button" might be 0% interest and even though the price is higher because they lose the rebates when taking the 0% offer, they don't care because they have it in their mind that they don't want to pay interest on their car loan and the payment is the same or lower than if they bought the vehicle with the rebates and standard finance rates. I've seen many other salespeople making follow up calls only because the manager says they must do it so they're essentially just "checking the box." The way I see it, I'm at the dealership to sell cars so I why would I "short cut" my follow up? I look at all the details of what the customer would like to accomplish and do my best to give them a reason to come back. I must have the deal make sense to the customer or they will not come back and buy the car.

Follow up has been a very critical piece of my success as a car salesman for all the reasons I've written about in this chapter. Diligent follow up is what separates me from most of my competition. It takes hard work and dedication however the payoff is well worth it. I believe diligent follow up is a major contributing factor to my ability to gain be-back clients as well as retaining old sold clients as well as a major reason I've been able to earn double the average car sales person salary every year I've been in the business with the exception of my first year and a half in the business.

Epilogue/Conclusion

Writing this book has been a great experience for me as it has allowed me to look back on my career and realize what I've accomplished and how I accomplished it. I've tried to emphasize the key ingredients to my success and I'm sure there are many other tips and techniques I could have added. In no way do I believe I'm the world's greatest salesperson, or even close to the world's greatest car salesperson however I have earned over one million dollars doing it. I realize there are many other ways to make a great living and be successful however the car business is, as I mentioned at the very beginning of this book, a great career for an uneducated slouch. You might be thinking – this guy really has a low opinion of himself, however, please keep in mind that I am confident in myself and very proud of what I've accomplished. I'm not an Ivy League graduate, Fortune 500 CEO, world renowned physicist, or POTUS although I am very proud of the fact that I had the foresight to see the car business was a great opportunity to earn a good living. I got involved because I realized what an integral part of our society personal vehicles are and that most adults in the USA have one, therefore providing massive opportunity. What I realized very shortly after beginning my career was that being a car salesperson is basically running your own business with very little overhead costs. Investing in a nice wardrobe and getting to work are about it. Other than that, the dealership provides a phone, computer, inventory and training. All I needed to do was show up but what it really boils down to is that there is no substitute for hard work, dedication and executing a plan. In addition, I will be clear that to double the average car salesperson income is not easy. In addition to long hours at the dealership, many phone calls, text messages, emails, and training, there are other adverse factors that need to be overcome. Mostly psychological factors like dealing with a sales slump, demanding and critical managers, the occasional rude customer, and the fact that car salespeople have a bad reputation for being sleazy. One very big thing I've always focused on that I haven't mentioned yet in this book is that I have no shame in being a car salesperson. I always enter the showroom knowing that I'm not the stereotypical car salesperson because I'm honest, trustworthy, and truly want to provide my clients with the best experience they've ever had buying a car. I truly believe that my clients feel this vibe from me and that's why they buy from me and why I have earned over ONE MILLION DOLLARS SELLING CARS!

Acknowledgments

Thank you to my wife Beth and son Grant for their support and motivating me to get up every day and go to the dealership, as well as putting up with the long hours and many nights of me arriving home late in the evening.

Thank you to my Mom, (Priscilla) and Dad (Carl) for teaching me how to have a great sense of humor, creativity, be personable, and a tireless work ethic.

Thank you to my siblings – Christine, Melanie, Cathy and Ben – for teaching me how to deal with people.

Thank you to my father in law, Jim Schirott for giving me the idea and motivating me to write this book.

Thank you to all the porters that I've worked with and that have been so helpful to me. There are too many to name however I must mention Manny Diaz, he is the best of the best.

About the Author

William Heussner had the vision to realize the opportunities retail automotive sales could offer and has generated over one million dollars of income, one car deal at a time. He has ranked in the top 100 Sales Consultants in the United States for the brand he sells, earned annual recognition awards 9 times for his brand, earned Salesman of the Year three times at one of the largest luxury car dealerships in Illinois and has developed a massive client base of repeat customers. Through hard work, enthusiasm, and dedication to the profession and his clients, he has had a successful and rewarding career as an automotive retail sales consultant.

William lives in Wheaton IL with his wife Beth and son Grant. In his free time, he enjoys spending time with his family, cooking, yard work and fishing. And a couple of cold pints of beer here and there, just to take the edge off.

www.ingramcontent.com/pod-product-compliance
Lightning Source LLC
Chambersburg PA
CBHW030719220526
45463CB00005B/2110